The Renaissance
THINKERS

With HISTORY PROJECTS for Kids

Diane C. Taylor

Nomad Press
A division of Nomad Communications
10 9 8 7 6 5 4 3 2 1

This book was manufactured by Friesens Book Division
Altona, MB, Canada
October 2018, Job #246316

ISBN Softcover: 978-1-61930-694-3
ISBN Hardcover: 978-1-61930-692-9

Educational Consultant, Marla Conn

Questions regarding the ordering of this book should be addressed to
Nomad Press
2456 Christian St.
White River Junction, VT 05001
www.nomadpress.net

Printed in Canada.

Titles in *The Renaissance for Kids* Series

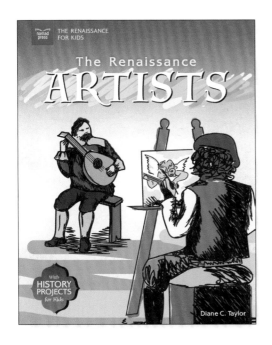

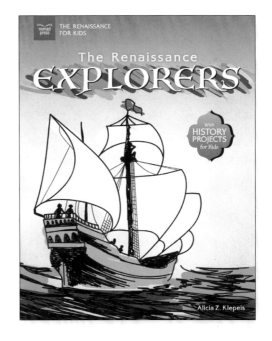

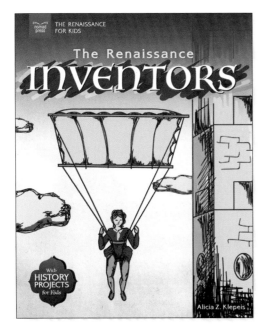

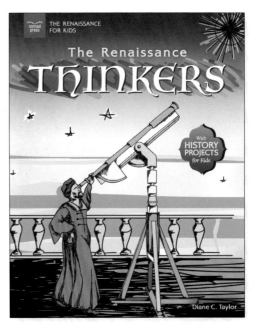

Check out more titles at www.nomadpress.net

TABLE OF
Contents

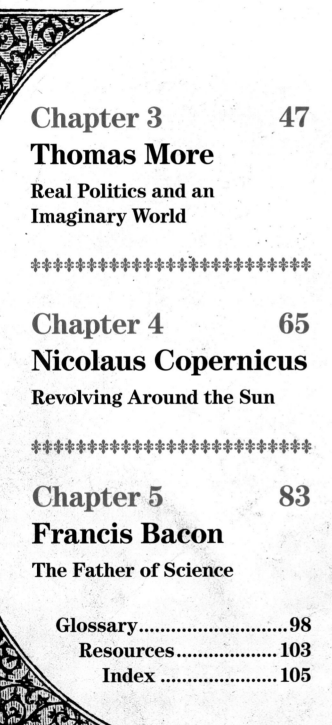

WHAT IS THE
Renaissance?

Vanitas

By Harmen Steenwijck,
circa 1640

The story of humanity covers tens of thousands of years. It reaches into the far distant past before humans made tools or learned to write. It includes our modern times, when we make computer chips and communicate with one another through text messages. Between those two extremes of human history lies a period we call the Renaissance. It's a sliver of time of about 400 years, from the 1300s through the 1600s.

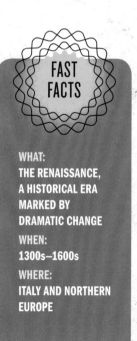

FAST FACTS

WHAT:
THE RENAISSANCE,
A HISTORICAL ERA
MARKED BY
DRAMATIC CHANGE

WHEN:
1300s–1600s

WHERE:
ITALY AND NORTHERN
EUROPE

We can trace the roots of the Renaissance to Florence, Italy, and watch it spread geographically into northern and western Europe. But the Renaissance was about more than change in certain cities and countries.

The Renaissance is about a change in a way of thinking that affected people across the globe. During the Renaissance, people loved learning about new ideas and having their old ideas challenged and changed. They were thirsty for knowledge about art, biology, mathematics, astronomy, chemistry, literature—everything!

They were eager to learn and experience new things and new ways of thinking and doing things.

Does it sound like an interesting time to live? Let's take a closer look at what types of change people experienced during the Renaissance.

> **"It is an unscrupulous intellect that does not pay to antiquity its due reverence."**
>
> **DESIDERIUS ERASMUS (1466–1536), CATHOLIC PRIEST AND RENAISSANCE HUMANIST**

Changing Times

What changes took place during the Renaissance? Let's take a look at three examples.

1. Economic Change

Most people in the Renaissance were farmers and lived in the countryside. The farmers, also called peasants, worked the land and paid their rent to the landowner, but they did this very differently from how we pay rent today.

Renaissance
1300s–1600s

1340s—50s
The bubonic plague kills people across Europe. In some places, almost half the population dies, and in others, nearly everyone survives.

1455
Johannes Gutenberg produces the first printed Bible, called the Gutenberg Bible, in Germany.

1493
Christopher Columbus sails to what Europeans will call the New World.

1517
Martin Luther protests against the Catholic Church, starting the movement known as the Reformation.

ITALIAE VETE=RIS SPECIMEN.

A map of Italy from 1584

"Man is the measure of all things."

PROTAGORAS (481–411 BCE), GREEK PHILOSOPHER

1522
The first circumnavigation of the globe, begun by Ferdinand Magellan's fleet, is completed by Juan Sebastian Elcano.

1531
Henry VIII breaks from the Catholic Church. He names himself head of the new Church of England.

1610
Galileo Galilei introduces a powerful new telescope and discovers the four moons of Jupiter.

1665
The first scientific journal is published in England.

1687
Isaac Newton uses mathematics to prove universal gravitation.

What other historical time periods have you heard about? How do they help us understand the entire history of human events?

Pieter Bruegel the Elder's *The Wedding Dance*, **1566, shows a glimpse of peasant life during the 1500s**

Usually, they would be able to keep much of the product of their work for themselves, but they would also owe the landowner—the lord— payment of some kind. In return for their use of the land, peasants could grow crops, raise livestock, and even provide military or household service for the lord.

By 1700, more people were becoming hired laborers. This meant that families slowly moved off the land to go to work in small businesses in towns. They might even move to new parts of the world to find new opportunities.

2. Religious Revolution

The Middle Ages was the period of time that came before the Renaissance. Throughout the Middle Ages, the Catholic Church played an enormous role in European life.

The pope, the head of the Catholic Church, was like a king. He controlled Italian territories known as the Papal States. He raised armies, waged wars, and made laws. He was also responsible for the spiritual well-being of people all around Europe. People cared deeply about what would happen to their souls if they died, so it was very important to them that they obeyed the decisions of the pope and the guidelines decided on by church leaders.

> **"Every man must do two things alone; he must do his own believing and his own dying."**
>
> **MARTIN LUTHER (1483–1546), WHO LEFT THE CATHOLIC CHURCH AND FOUNDED THE PROTESTANT LUTHERAN CHURCH**

In the later Middle Ages, in the fourteenth and fifteenth centuries, people had lots of different options for how they could live the best Christian life. Some people became monks, nuns, or priests, while others lived a religious life without taking religious vows. Other people remained part of the secular world, but would often give money for prayers and donate to the poor, particularly as they grew older.

This woodcut shows life in the Middle Ages, a period when the Church held power over everyone, from a 1898 book by Edward Lewes Cutts.

Especially in the sixteenth century, after Martin Luther and other reformers started to question the organization of the Church and which beliefs were most true, people had even more religious options. They even fought wars over which beliefs were correct!

By 1650, people usually had two choices: follow the religion of their ruler—even if it meant converting to another religion—or move to a different land where they agreed with the ruler's religion.

3. Technological Change

Technology took off in many new directions during the Renaissance. But the printing press might have been the most revolutionary innovation of all. Developed by Johannes Gutenberg (c. 1400–1468) of Germany, the printing press made it possible to mass produce books. As books became readily available, more people learned to read. New ideas spread faster than ever.

CONNECT

You can see pictures of a Gutenberg Bible, the first book printed on a printing press, at an online exhibit from the University of Texas at Austin.

🔍 Texas Gutenberg

SHIPS AHOY!

Christopher Columbus (c. 1451–1506) was just one of many notable Renaissance explorers whose discoveries challenged what people thought they knew about the world. Their voyages brought Europeans all over the world, where they founded colonies and encountered new cultures, foods, and ways of living, forever changing the course of human history.

Daring to Discover

The Renaissance was a change that took place within the human mind. Educated men and women developed a sharp interest in the cultures of ancient Greece and Rome, which had thrived more than a thousand years before.

They went in search of ancient books, art, and architecture. What they found introduced them to whole new ways of thinking.

Didn't people read ancient texts during the Middle Ages? Educated people, rulers, and priests did, but books were hard to come by.

Because people did not have access to lots of books, most people developed really good memories—they could recite multiple-hour poems without reading them! Educated people also kept records of events that happened, diplomatic and financial agreements, and wrote explanations of the Bible and other texts. By the time of the Renaissance, even people who couldn't read would hold onto documents that gave them special rights—they'd just have someone else read them!

Today, you can go to a library and find plenty of free books, you can go to a bookstore to buy books, or even find books online. But during the Middle Ages, most books were hidden away in monasteries. You couldn't just take one home with you. You had to make a copy of it—by hand.

Humanism

The ancient Greeks and Romans asked big questions. What is the meaning of life? How does the world work? What is freedom? What is beauty? What is justice?

Portrait de Pythagore d'après l'antique.

maréchal: del.   *Dambrun. sculp.*

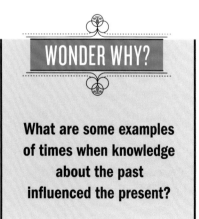

WONDER WHY?

What are some examples of times when knowledge about the past influenced the present?

Pythagoras was an ancient Greek thinker who came up with a rule about right triangles called the Pythagorean Theorem.

Line engraving by Jean Dambrun after Maréchal

credit: Wellcome Collection (CC BY 4.0)

7

In the Middle Ages, scholars studied how they could make the Bible and other religious texts fit together with ancient thought. Sometimes, this was easy, sometimes, hard, but they believed that all of the writings of intelligent men were looking for the same godly truth.

During the Renaissance, people called humanists were more interested in finding and studying the original versions of texts. They began to realize that every author and every text needed to be understood within its own unique context. This led them to interpret writings in different ways than scholars before them.

Later thinkers were inspired by humanist writings to ask different questions about the world in which they lived. How did the natural world operate? What was the relationship between humans and the rest of the world?

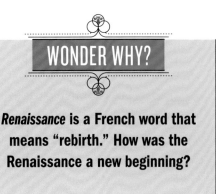

WONDER WHY?

Renaissance is a French word that means "rebirth." How was the Renaissance a new beginning?

"Cultivation to the mind is as necessary as food to the body."

MARCUS TILLIUS CICERO (106–43 BCE), ROMAN LAWYER AND POLITICIAN

The Thinkers

In *The Renaissance Thinkers*, you will meet five Renaissance humanists who thought outside the box.

+ **Filippo Brunelleschi** solved major problems in architecture.

+ **Niccolò Machiavelli** wrote groundbreaking books about politics.

+ **Nicolaus Copernicus** worked out accurate measurements of the earth in relation to the sun.

+ **Thomas More** wrote a book of social and political satire.

+ **Francis Bacon** argued for an approach to scientific research based on observation and reason.

You'll also meet many other philosophers and scientists, including women and people of color, who were curious about the world around them. Let's get started!

Make a Culture Collage

One of the terms we use to describe the years in Europe from the 1300s through the 1600s is the *Renaissance*. What words or phrases could you use that define the era we live in right now? Make a culture collage and see if you can find one.

> ➤ **Think about the culture we live in today.** What does our society value? What do we think is important? How do we show our values?

> ➤ **Look through magazines, newspapers, and websites for images that show the values of today's society.** You might include pictures of politicians, movie stars, refugees, wars, scientists, artists, and writers. What about animals, places, and things?

> ➤ **Group your pictures under a variety of cultural categories, such as art, science, technology, religion, politics, business, and music.** Arrange your images into a poster board collage.

> ➤ **Study your collage.** Do your images suggest a theme of any kind? Can you think of a word or phrase that sums up what your collage represents? What kind of era do we live in today?

WORDS OF WONDER

This book is packed with lots of new vocabulary! Try figuring out the meanings of unfamiliar words using the context and roots of the words. There is a glossary in the back to help you and Words of Wonder check-ins for every chapter.

CONNECT

The Republic is a famous work of Greek philosophy. Written by Plato in 360 BCE, it describes a conversation among friends. Take a look at it here. Why do you think Plato wrote his ideas as a fictional conversation?

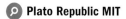 **Plato Republic MIT**

A statue of Brunelleschi near the Santa Maria del Fiore, looking up at the dome he designed

CHAPTER 1

FILIPPO
Brunelleschi

When you look at a photograph of Florence, Italy, you're likely to see a large, orange-colored dome. That's the top of the Florence Cathedral, or the Santa Maria del Fiore. It's one of the great tourist attractions of Europe. More than 4 million people visit it every year.

A bust of Brunelleschi

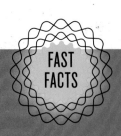

FAST FACTS

BIRTH DATE: 1377

PLACE OF BIRTH:
FLORENCE, ITALY

AGE AT DEATH: 69

PLACE OF BURIAL:
FLORENCE CATHEDRAL

FAMOUS ACCOMPLISHMENTS:
- **REDISCOVERY OF LINEAR PERSPECTIVE**

- **CONSTRUCTION OF THE DOME ON THE FLORENCE CATHEDRAL**

- **INNOVATIVE ENGINEERING OF CONSTRUCTION MATERIALS AND EQUIPMENT**

The Florence Cathedral

Without one man, Filippo Brunelleschi, that dome might not exist. It took hundreds of years—and a man trained as a goldsmith—for the Florence Cathedral dome to go from being an idea to a reality.

> **"I propose to build for eternity."**
>
> **FILIPPO BRUNELLESCHI**

Brunelleschi
1377–1446

1377
Brunelleschi is born in Florence, in the neighborhood of the Santa Maria del Fiore.

1398
Brunelleschi becomes a master goldsmith.

1401
He loses a competition to create the bronze doors of the baptistery in Florence.

1401
Brunelleschi moves to Rome and spends many hours studying the ancient ruins there.

Early Years

Filippo Brunelleschi was the middle child of a lawyer father, Brunellesco di Lippo (dates unknown), and his wife, Giuliana Spini (dates unknown). Brunelleschi's family and friends called him "Pippo." At first, Pippo's parents wanted him to become a lawyer, just like his dad. But Brunelleschi was more interested in art, so when he was a teenager, his parents apprenticed him to a goldsmith.

CONNECT

Watch a video about goldsmiths during the Renaissance and today. Why do you think this artistic tradition has survived all these centuries?

🔍 **Rai goldsmith Tuscany**

As a goldsmith, Brunelleschi made jewelry, such as buttons and belt buckles, necklaces and rings. During the Renaissance, a goldsmith was required to master a wide range of artistic skills, and Brunelleschi also learned to draw, engrave, sculpt, and work with molten metal.

By the time Brunelleschi was a master goldsmith at age 21, he was capable of taking on many art-related assignments. Although he later gained fame as an architect and engineer, he never received any formal education in either field.

WONDER WHY?

Many cities are associated with beautiful and famous buildings. Can you think of any in the United States, Europe, Africa, or Asia? What do these grand structures tell us about their home cities or countries? Why do we feel they are worth the time, money, and effort to construct?

1418
Brunelleschi wins the competition to erect the dome of the Santa Maria del Fiore, despite the lack of explanation for the plans he offers.

1419
Brunelleschi designs the Ospedale degli Innocenti, an orphanage and the first new building in Florence with Romanesque features.

1421
Brunelleschi demonstrates linear perspective.

1421
Construction on the Florence Cathedral dome begins.

1442
Construction begins on the Pazzi Chapel in Florence, another of Brunelleschi's Romanesque buildings.

1446
Brunelleschi dies at age 69.

Competitors in Florence

Three years after he became a master goldsmith, Brunelleschi entered an important competition. The Florence Cathedral complex included the San Giovanni Baptistery, a religious building where children in Florence were baptized.

Civic leaders in Florence decided to adorn the baptistery with a new set of elaborate bronze doors. They sent out a call for artists to submit their ideas.

The Gates of Paradise by Lorenzo Ghiberti, 1425

Brunelleschi's model is on the right and Ghiberti's is on the left.

Brunelleschi was one of seven artists to submit model bronze doors to the contest. In 1402, a committee of 34 people narrowed the contestants to two artists—Brunelleschi and another young goldsmith named Lorenzo Ghiberti (1378–1455).

The committee members admired both models and struggled to choose just one winner. They decided that the two goldsmiths could work on the project together. Brunelleschi, however, refused to work with another artist, so the job went to Ghiberti.

Brunelleschi in Rome

Even though he didn't accept the project, Brunelleschi won fame for the beauty and craftsmanship of his bronze models for the baptistery. Still, he was angry about the way the competition had played out. He vowed never to work in bronze sculpture again— and he never did.

He also decided to leave Florence. He moved to Rome, Italy, where he lived, on and off, for the next 13 years. He supported himself making jewelry, but what really interested Brunelleschi was architecture. Roman architects had constructed some of the largest and most complex buildings of the ancient world. Brunelleschi wanted to unravel the mysteries of how they had done it.

"Filippo di Ser Brunellesco
. . . was small in stature
. . . but great in genius."

GIORGIO VASARI (1511-1574),
LIVES OF THE ARTISTS

Ancient ruins dotted the Roman landscape. Frequently accompanied by his friend, the Florentine sculptor Donatello (1386–1466), Brunelleschi explored the remnants of Rome's great buildings. He didn't know it at the time, but those explorations would change his life.

**Roman ruins,
The Forum**

Linear Perspective

While Brunelleschi was in Rome, he made detailed drawings of the ancient ruins. In the process, he rediscovered a lost artistic technique known as linear perspective. It's a technique that allows artists to portray three-dimensional objects on a two-dimensional surface.

What does that mean?

Picture a piece of paper. A piece of paper is a flat, two-dimensional plane. It has height and width. But we view the world in three dimensions—height, width, and depth. So, if we can create the illusion of depth in a drawing or painting, objects look more realistic.

Some ancient Roman and Greek artists had known how to do that, but they often did not use linear perspective because they wanted to focus on things such as the importance of a person, rather than his or her location in a scene. By the early 1400s, that knowledge had been lost—until Brunelleschi rediscovered it.

CONNECT

Watch a reenactment of Brunelleschi's demonstration of linear perspective.

 Khan Brunelleschi experiment

FAMILY AFFAIRS

Brunelleschi never married and he was never named as the biological father of any children, but he did have the equivalent of an adopted son. Known familiarly as "Il Buggiano," Andrea Cavalcanti (1412–1462) was a sculptor Brunelleschi took on as an assistant. Buggiano worked on important commissions for his master, but his relationship to Brunelleschi must have been more than that of just another employee. Buggiano was named an heir in Brunelleschi's will. The two men, however, were not always on good terms. When Buggiano was 22, Brunelleschi failed to pay him a substantial amount of money. Buggiano responded by stealing the money and escaping to Naples, Italy. Brunelleschi arranged for authorities in Naples to return the younger man to Florence. After he arrived home, he continued to work for Brunelleschi for many years.

The Florence Demonstration

Brunelleschi learned to establish a single vanishing point on a piece of paper, and to make all horizontal lines in his drawing meet at that one point on the "horizon." The result was the illusion of three-dimensional objects on a flat surface.

In 1421, Brunelleschi staged a brilliant demonstration of linear perspective in Florence. He set up an easel 115 feet away from the front of the baptistery and painted, in perfect perspective, what he saw. He made a small hole in the painting, right at the vanishing point, and then turned the painting away from his viewers.

He had people hold up a mirror in front of the painted side of the artwork while they looked through the hole from the blank side. What they saw astonished them. The reflection of Brunelleschi's painting in the mirror looked exactly like the real baptistery. As they glanced from the mirror to the actual building, they could hardly tell the difference between illusion and reality.

Brunelleschi had reopened the doors onto perspective and changed the art and architecture worlds forever.

The Problem

In 1418, city leaders in Florence had a problem. The Santa Maria del Fiore had been under construction since 1294. It was supposed to be the pride of the city. But the job had never been finished.

What was the holdup? The dome.

WONDER WHY?

Architecture has changed since Brunelleschi's time, but domes are still with us. Where in the American landscape do you see domes today? What kinds of domes are being made? What do they represent?

The original architects had designed it to be the tallest and widest vaulted structure in the world. It was supposed to rise 170 feet from the ground and have a diameter of more than 143 feet.

The problem was, nobody knew how to build such a dome.

A dome that large had not been constructed since the Pantheon in ancient Rome. But the ancient architectural methods had been lost.

Fortunately, Brunelleschi's studies of Roman ruins paved the way to a solution. When city leaders called for artists to submit construction plans for the dome, Brunelleschi accepted the challenge.

CONNECT

Take a virtual tour of the Pantheon.

🔍 vimeo Pantheon

A Dome Like No Other

The dome of the Florence Cathedral presented many challenges.

City leaders wanted it to be big, but they also wanted it to stand out from other cathedrals throughout Europe. They wanted a dome that didn't use Gothic-style flying buttresses. Buttresses are structures that prop up a large building and keep it from collapsing under its own weight. You can see them in photographs of the Notre Dame Cathedral in Paris, France.

They also wanted the dome to be made without wooden supports. Even today, stone or brick domes are built with wooden supports that are removed once construction is finished. But in Renaissance Italy, wood was hard to come by. Getting enough wood to complete the dome of the Florence Cathedral was out of the question.

Flying buttresses of Notre Dame Cathedral

credit: Matthias Zirngibl (CC BY 2.0)

> "So astonishing was the plan that many of Filippo's contemporaries considered him a lunatic."
>
> **ROSS KING (1962–), *BRUNELLESCHI'S DOME***

Lifting building materials hundreds of feet into the air presented another challenge. Materials had never been lifted to such a tremendous height before in Italy. And once large stones were lifted up, how would they be set in place? How would this be done today?

THE BABBLER

Brunelleschi always feared that someone would take credit for his inventions. As a result, he kept a lot of secrets. When he submitted his design for the cathedral dome, for example, he refused to explain exactly how he planned to construct it.

The committee responsible for the construction of the dome pressed him for details, but he wouldn't budge. At one point during a meeting, people became so frustrated that they physically tossed Brunelleschi out of the room. They angrily referred to him as "an ass and a babbler."

Why they eventually gave the job to Brunelleschi remains a mystery to this day. He did create a model dome to show what he had in mind, but he never submitted any of his plans in writing. Would you have trusted him to accomplish what he claimed he could?

How Did He Do It?

Because Brunelleschi never wrote down his architectural or engineering designs, historians have struggled for centuries to unravel the secrets of his success. And we still don't completely understand how he accomplished what no one else has ever been able to do.

However, we do know some of his methods. Here are some of his most significant innovations:

+ creation of a stone chain,

+ development of new bricks,

+ design and construction of a revolutionary new hoist and crane.

The Chain of Stone

To keep the dome from collapsing under its own weight, Brunelleschi devised four elaborate sets of chains made of stone. They resembled railroad tracks. They had two long stone beams intersected with smaller stone beams. The stone chains hugged the circumference of the dome.

Have you ever seen a barrel made of wooden staves and iron rings? The iron rings hold the staves together so the barrel doesn't fall apart. The chains of stone worked much the same way around the dome as iron rings.

The Bricks

To build the dome of the Florence Cathedral, Brunelleschi oversaw the production of nearly 4 million bricks. During the Renaissance in Florence, most bricks were made to a standard size of 10 by 5 inches. But Brunelleschi needed bricks of different shapes and sizes. He created molds for triangular bricks, dovetail bricks, and bricks with flanges, or ridges.

WONDER WHY?

The lever, wheel and axle, pulley, inclined plane, wedge, and screw are all known as simple machines. Can you think of any of these that you use in daily life? Do you ever use a fork?

> **"Do not share your inventions with many; share them only with the few who understand and love the sciences."**
>
> **FILIPPO BRUNELLESCHI**

Why did Brunelleschi need all these different bricks? He had figured out a new pattern for laying bricks that allowed him to build the dome without supports.

The Hoist

A hoist lifts heavy objects using a series of ropes and pulleys. Hoists had been used in construction for thousands of years, and they had been powered by human beings! Can you imagine walking inside a giant hamster wheel to generate energy? That's how hoists were supplied with power before Brunelleschi came on the scene.

No hoist of the 1400s could lift the enormous beams of Brunelleschi's stone chain. So, Brunelleschi invented a new one that was more technologically advanced than any hoist from the previous 3,000 years.

First, to power his machine, Brunelleschi switched from men to oxen. This saved men from a torturous job, and also allowed for much heavier loads to be lifted.

Second, he introduced reversible gears. These allowed workers to raise a load up, switch gears, and send another load back down— without having to unhitch an ox and start it walking in the opposite direction. It was a revolutionary timesaver, allowing the hoist to lift one load every 10 minutes.

Drawing of Brunelleschi's hoist, driven by a horse rather than an ox

The Crane

Getting huge stone beams to the top of the dome was one challenge. Setting them in place was another.

For that task, Brunelleschi designed a new crane called a castello. Like the hoist, it was made of wood. It allowed workers to move the massive stone beams by slight degrees up, down, and sideways.

CONNECT

Visit the Florence Cathedral!

 Khan Florence Cathedral

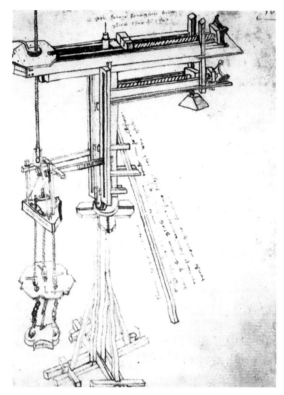

 Drawing of Brunelleschi's crane, the castello

Drawings by Leonardo da Vinci of a three-speed winch developed by Brunelleschi

Brunelleschi's Rivals

Brunelleschi was not the only person to submit plans for construction of the dome. Among several others, his old rival, Lorenzo Ghiberti, made a model and offered plans as well. This time, however, he lost to Brunelleschi.

But that didn't bring an end to their competitive relationship. The dome committee later appointed two more people to share equal responsibility with Brunelleschi—none other than Ghiberti and a poet named Giovanni da Prato (dates unknown).

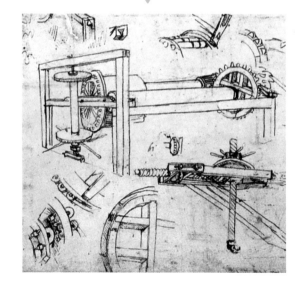

The Great Mosque in Djenné
credit: Jurgen (CC BY 2.0)

WONDER WHY?

Brunelleschi was awarded one of the first patents in the world, which means he legally owned everything about his idea for an invention. Why do inventors patent their ideas? Do you know other inventors—past or present—who have patented their work?

ISLAMIC ARCHITECTURE IN AFRICA

Brunelleschi would have preferred to work alone. But he controlled his anger and stuck with the project. Throughout the following two decades, Ghiberti and Prato tried several times to discredit Brunelleschi, but the genius always prevailed. He repeatedly proved that he was the best man for the job.

The Final Competition

The finishing touch on the dome of the Florence Cathedral was the design and installation of a lantern. This would add a final piece of decoration to the structure and also serve the practical purpose of letting in sunlight.

Throughout Europe, for hundreds of years people created elaborate cathedrals to honor their Christian god. During that same time period, especially in northern Africa and what's now Spain and Portugal, Muslims created elaborate mosques to honor their Islamic god. The continent of Africa covers an enormous area, and architectural styles vary greatly from one end of the continent to the other. As in most other places, the design and construction of African mosques was influenced by both outside forces and local traditions. Part of the reason why many cultures influenced the design and construction of African mosques is that Islam was introduced to Africa from Middle Eastern areas, such as present-day Saudi Arabia.

Unlike the Florence Cathedral, domes did not figure heavily in African mosques. Nonetheless, they were grand, imposing structures. In the country of Mali, for example, the Great Mosque in the town of Djenné is the largest clay building in the world. Originally constructed in the 1200s, it was recreated in 1907 and named a UNESCO World Heritage Site in 1988.

Once again, in 1436, Brunelleschi found himself competing against Ghiberti. Once again, Brunelleschi won the contest. But the competition for the cathedral lantern pitted Brunelleschi against other contenders as well, including a devious carpenter named Antonio di Ciaccheri Manetti (1402–1460). Brunelleschi hired Manetti to construct wooden models of his lanterns only to see Manetti submit the designs as his own!

The ruse ultimately failed. But Brunelleschi had to watch Manetti submit several variations of his own lantern before cathedral committee members finally caught on to what was happening.

❧ PLAUTILLA BRICCI (1616-1690) ❧

Two hundred years after Brunelleschi's death, Renaissance Europe saw the rise of its first female architect. Very little is known about Plautilla Bricci, other than that she was born in Rome and most likely learned her trade alongside her architect brother Basilio. Documents show, however, that in 1665 she was the sole architect of a villa near Porta San Pancrazio. You can still see the chapel she designed in the church of San Luigi dei Francesi in Rome.

> "On account of the extraordinary gifts of his mind and his unique abilities, the body lain below in this soil is commanded to be interred by a grateful land."
>
> BRUNELLESCHI'S EPITAPH, POSTED INSIDE THE FLORENCE CATHEDRAL

Brunelleschi's Legacy

Filippo Brunelleschi worked on the Florence Cathedral for more than 25 years. Sadly, he never saw the dome in its final glory. The lantern was not finished until 1461, which was 15 years after his death, and the lantern was not topped with a gilded copper ball and a cross until 1469.

Brunelleschi had died after a brief illness in 1446.

From start to finish, it took more than 170 years to complete the Florence Cathedral. Countless hands contributed to the effort, from the original architects to the masons who climbed hundreds of steps to begin work each day high up on the curved vault of the dome.

The interior of Brunelleschi's dome

credit: tpholland
(CC BY 2.0)

Still, no one was more crucial to this grand human endeavor than Brunelleschi. The dome is still the largest stone structure in the world. And even today, to honor his achievements, the citizens of Florence always hold a parade on the anniversary of Brunelleschi's death. Dressed in period costumes, they wind through the streets of Florence until they reach his burial site at the cathedral.

WORDS OF WONDER

What vocabulary words did you discover? Can you figure out the meanings of these words by using the context and roots? Look in the glossary for help!

architect · buttress circumference · linear perspective patent · simple machine

Project

The Arch of History

Human beings have used arches in their construction designs since the time of ancient Mesopotamia more than 3,000 years ago. But it was the ancient Romans who first perfected the architectural use of arches, and it was from the Romans that Brunelleschi learned to construct the dome of the Florence Cathedral.

➤ **Conduct internet and library research about the history of arches, from the time of the ancient Romans to modern times.** Consider these questions.

- How many categories of arches are there?
- What are some of the ways that arches can be constructed?
- How have arches changed and developed throughout history?
- In addition to buildings, what other structures are created with arches?

- What are some of the most famous arches in the world? Where are they located? What do they represent?
- What prevents an arch from collapsing? This is the toughest thing to understand about arches. Keep your explanation simple, but give it your best shot!

➤ **Now try to build your own arch!** Create a model out of supplies you find around your house and school, such as blocks, recycled boxes and cans, popsicle sticks, stones, and anything else you can think of!

➤ **Test the stability of your arch by resting items on top of it.** Can your arch hold up a little car? An apple? A book? How can you make it stronger without adding too much material?

CONNECT

Watch people try to build an arch without supports at the St. Louis Science Center. Do you think you could do it?

🔍 **Neon Guy arch video**

Exploring Architecture

Architectural styles vary a great deal from one culture to the next and across the centuries of human history. Buildings serve practical purposes, but they are also a form of art that can be as expressive as a painting or a sculpture. Let's dive deeper into a work of architecture!

➤ **Is there a famous building you would like to visit?** Why or why not? Have you already visited a famous building, such as the White House in Washington, DC, the Empire State Building in New York City, or the famous Hearst Mansion in California?

➤ **Conduct internet and library research about a famous building and create a presentation of your findings.** Your presentation should include both written and visual elements and answer the following questions.

- What was the building's original purpose? Was it a home, a business, a public building, or something else?

- Where and when was it constructed? Who paid to have it erected?

- What was the building's main construction material?

- Who was the main architect? What other buildings had the architect done before taking on this project?

- What is the architectural style of the building? Is it modern, colonial, Victorian, or something else?

- What does this building reveal about the culture in which it was produced?

- What do you feel when you look at this building or think about walking around inside of it?

- Is this a building you want to visit? Why or why not?

➤ **Share your presentation with classmates or friends.** What kinds of buildings did others choose to explore? What do the various buildings reveal about the people who created them?

CONNECT

Watch another kind of dome being made—an igloo!

 Kids Should see igloo

Portrait of Niccolò Machiavelli

By Santi di Tito

CHAPTER 2

NICCOLÒ
Machiavelli

Statue of Machiavelli
By Lorenzo Bartolini

Very few people do anything so noteworthy that their last name takes on a new meaning after they die. But that's what happened to Niccolò Machiavelli—and not in a good way, either. The word "Machiavelli" stands for nearly everything bad in politics. Lying, cheating, scheming, backstabbing, killing—those are all qualities associated with Machiavellianism.

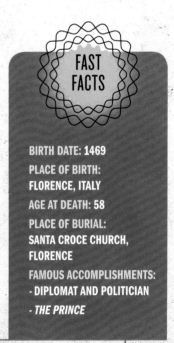

FAST FACTS

BIRTH DATE: **1469**

PLACE OF BIRTH:
FLORENCE, ITALY

AGE AT DEATH: **58**

PLACE OF BURIAL:
**SANTA CROCE CHURCH,
FLORENCE**

FAMOUS ACCOMPLISHMENTS:
- **DIPLOMAT AND POLITICIAN**
- *THE PRINCE*

What did Niccolò Machiavelli do to receive such a bad reputation? Even though he wrote many works (plays, histories, and political treatises), he is most famous for a small book called *The Prince*. During the 500 years since it was written, *The Prince* has been translated into dozens of languages and been read by millions of people. It has turned Machiavelli's name into a description of bad behavior and made the man himself one of the most controversial figures in history. Let's take a look and see how this happened!

Early Years

Niccolò Machiavelli was the third child and first son of a family where the humanist ideals of the Renaissance were highly valued. Not much is known about his mother, Bartolomea (1441–1496), but his father, Bernardo (1428–1500), was a lawyer with a great interest in the books and philosophy of the ancient Greeks and Romans. He collected, read, and translated them.

His father made sure that Machiavelli received a humanist education. It started with formal training in Latin when he was seven and continued with studies at a university founded by a leading humanist scholar named Cristoforo Landino (1424–1498). At Landino's school, Machiavelli studied public speaking, grammar, poetry, history, and moral philosophy.

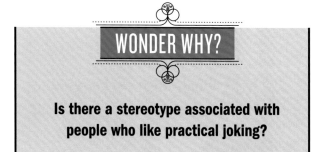

WONDER WHY?

Is there a stereotype associated with people who like practical joking?

His life wasn't all hard work and studying, though. When Machiavelli was young, his friends nicknamed him "Macchia," an Italian word for "smear" or "stain." That doesn't sound very nice. *Macchia* actually referred to the "stain" left on a person who had been the recipient of one of Niccolò's practical jokes.

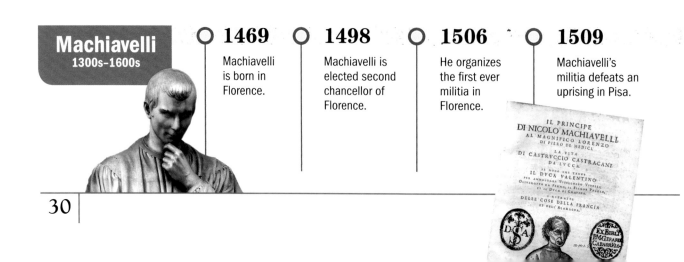

Machiavelli
1300s–1600s

1469
Machiavelli is born in Florence.

1498
Machiavelli is elected second chancellor of Florence.

1506
He organizes the first ever militia in Florence.

1509
Machiavelli's militia defeats an uprising in Pisa.

NICCOLÒ MACHIAVELLI

✳✳

"I have met a creature so gracious, so refined, so noble . . . that never could either my praise or my love for her be as much as she deserves."

MACHIAVELLI IN A LETTER TO VETTORI, DESCRIBING AN EXTRAMARITAL GIRLFRIEND IN 1514

Angel Appearing to Zacharias

By Domenico Ghirlandaio (1448–1494), between 1486 and 1490. Shows Cristofo Landino, center, facing the viewer. Landino's school was a major influence in Machiavelli's life.

1512
The Medici return to power in Florence. Machiavelli is imprisoned and tortured.

1513
Machiavelli retreats to the countryside and writes *The Prince.*

1516
He presents *The Prince* to Lorenzo di Piero de' Medici.

1520
Machiavelli begins writing his history of Florence.

1521
He resumes work as a diplomat for the Medici.

1527
Medici are expelled from Florence. Machiavelli dies in Florence.

One of the texts that Machiavelli often read and in which he wrote many notes in the margins was *On the Nature of Things* (*De Rerum Natura*), a 7,400-line poem written in Latin by the Roman philosopher Lucretius (c. 99–55 BCE). This popular poem was rediscovered by Poggio Bracciolini (1380–1459) after it had been lost for hundreds of years.

Many thinkers spent time during the next few decades correcting the only copy of this manuscript that still existed. By the time Machiavelli studied this text, other thinkers had already edited it so that it was as close to the original as they could make it.

First Job

Machiavelli was 29 when he became an administrator and diplomat for the city of Florence. This was an elected position known as second chancellor. It was a prestigious job, but Machiavelli was certainly qualified. Government business was conducted in Latin, which he had been reading, writing, and speaking since he was a child.

The first page of *On the Nature of Things* by Lucretius, 1483

credit: Ed Suominen (CC BY 2.0)

Equally important were Machiavelli's skills as a public speaker and his knowledge of history. A big part of his job was to persuade a wide range of European leaders to act in ways that benefitted Florence. He had to think fast on his feet, speak well, and understand complicated history to know which countries were Florence's friends and which were its enemies.

CONNECT

You can listen to a few stanzas of *On the Nature of Things* at this website. How is this poem different from others you have read or heard?

🔍 **nature things Vimont**

Renaissance Italy was made up of dozens of city-states and a few kingdoms and duchies. These were essentially small countries. The most powerful were Milan and Venice in the north, Naples in the south, the Papal States in the middle, and Florence in the west.

Relations among the city-states were nearly always tense with conflict. They constantly battled one another for territory and power.

RENAISSANCE WARFARE

Renaissance wars were both frequent and extremely complicated. They were most often fought by mercenary armies. These were bands of noncitizen soldiers hired to conduct warfare on behalf of a city-state. Florence, for example, might hire a mercenary army of soldiers from Switzerland to wage a war against a mercenary army of soldiers from Spain, who were fighting on behalf of the French. Battles in the Renaissance were also very deadly. The leaders of mercenary armies, called the *condottieri*, often led troops that were brutal to the people who lived in the area. These troops sometimes killed innocent civilians if they were not paid their wages—they would take their wages from the property of the people. They destroyed homes, crops, and livestock, and set up lengthy blockades that drove entire populations to the brink of starvation.

WONDER WHY?

How would a constant fear of war affect a person's thinking? Would you think or feel differently if your town or country were likely to be invaded? Can you think of places in the world where this is a reality today?

Portrait of Giuliano de' Medici by Sandro Botticelli, circa 1478. Giuliano was the man murdered by a member of the Pazzi family.

Florentine Politics

Bloody battles of another sort also took place within the walls of Florence itself. In theory, Florence was ruled by elected leaders. In fact, even though these leaders were elected, the elections were controlled by wealthy families who fought one another for power. And assassination was a common way to deal with your enemies.

In 1478, for example, the Medici family controlled the elected government of Florence. The Pazzi family wanted to force them out, so the Pazzi clan attempted to assassinate two members of the Medici family. They killed one man and wounded another.

In the days after the attack, the Medici rounded up the assassins, killed them, and hung the bodies from the windows of a public building. The message was clear: An ugly fate awaited anyone who challenged the Medici.

Man in the Middle

In his role as second chancellor, Machiavelli was always trying to balance the needs of Florence against the demands of others. If a warlord demanded more money and Florence refused to pay it, it was Machiavelli who had to meet with the *condottiere* and find a way to resolve the problem.

If the king of France wanted Florence to help him invade the city-state of Naples, it was Machiavelli who traveled to the French court and tried to explain Florence's objections. Whatever the political situation, Machiavelli was always the man in the middle of two competing forces. It was a precarious situation to be in. Failure could result in war.

Handling political situations in Florence could be a tricky business. Machiavelli had many enemies who sought to undermine his position, especially when he was out of town.

They complained about Machiavelli's work habits and criticized his decisions when he was unable to defend himself in person. Fortunately, Machiavelli's friends wrote to him when he was away and kept him informed of what was happening behind his back.

CONNECT

Was the Renaissance really the Renaissance? Join John Green for a discussion on this time period.

🔍 **crash course renaissance**

One of his strongest allies at the chancellery was a man named Biagio Buonaccorsi (1472–1526). He not only kept Machiavelli aware of what was happening at work, but also let him know when trouble was brewing with his wife, Marietta, at home.

FAMILY AFFAIRS

Machiavelli married Marietta Corsini (dates unknown) when he was 32. The couple stayed together for the rest of Machiavelli's life, and they raised a family of seven children—two girls and five boys. But it was not an entirely happy marriage. Machiavelli's job as second chancellor took him away from home for long stretches of time, and Marietta missed him when he was gone. Marietta also had to accept that her husband was routinely unfaithful to her. Machiavelli was a frequent visitor to the brothels of Florence and Rome. He fell in and out of love on numerous occasions and carried on affairs that sometimes lasted for years.

DIPLOMACY ABROAD

Machiavelli's travels as a diplomat took him as far away as France and Germany. But the reach of diplomacy during the Renaissance extended far beyond the borders of Europe. Antonio Emanuele Ne Vunda (dates uncertain) was an extraordinary example of a diplomat traveling great distances to represent his country. He was an ambassador from the West African Kingdom of Kongo, sent by his king to meet with Pope Paul V (1550–1621). Ne Vunda's journey to Italy was a long one. It started in 1604, took him through Brazil and Spain, and ended in Rome in 1608. Believed to be the first African ambassador to Europe in history, Ne Vunda tragically died just two days after he arrived in Rome.

End of an Era

Despite political hazards both at home and abroad, Machiavelli kept his job as second chancellor for 15 years. But in 1512, his luck ran out.

The Medici family had been out of power and banned from Florence for the last 18 years. For the first four years after they were kicked out, a wildly popular preacher named Savonarola was the most influential man in Florence, influencing who held political office just like the Medici had. By 1512, however, the Medici stormed Florence with a mercenary army and took back control of the city. The Medici immediately cleaned house and got rid of anyone they considered an enemy. That included Machiavelli and Buouaccorsi. They both lost their jobs.

A painting that shows the Medici family members as the three wise men, between 1459 and 1464

By Benozzo Gozzoli

Members of the court of the Medici from the workshop of Bronzino (1503–1572)

But things got even worse for Machiavelli. The Medici suspected him of participating in an assassination plot. They imprisoned Machiavelli and tortured him. They set him free after a few days, but he was ordered to stay out of Florence for a year.

A Book as Job Application

Released from prison, Machiavelli retreated to his family's country estate outside of Florence. Even though the Medici had imprisoned and tortured him, Machiavelli still wanted to work for them, since they now controlled Florence. How would he get back into their good graces?

CONNECT

Explore Machiavelli's country estate as it is today!

🔍 **Machiavelli's villa**

He decided to write a book—one that would include everything he knew about how leaders throughout history had gained power and then either lost it or kept it. Since the Medici were newly returned to power, Machiavelli figured they would find his book useful. He hoped they would read it and offer him a job.

> "[I am] rotting away . . . unable to find any man who recalls my service or believes I might be good for anything."
>
> **MACHIAVELLI, LETTER TO VETTORI, JUNE 1513**

Mirrors for Princes

People had written guidebooks for rulers for hundreds of years. They were called "mirrors for princes," or *principum specula* in Latin, and they offered what seemed like good advice. Be honest. Be trustworthy. Be kind. Be generous. Avoid war. Keep your promises.

Many mirrors for princes had been written by religious leaders. They were as concerned with the eternal soul of a prince as they were with his earthly success. They spelled out how a leader ought to behave if he wanted to rule and not spend eternity in hell.

The End of Virtue

With *The Prince*, Machiavelli turned the traditions of the mirror book upside down. Machiavelli declared that "(A) prince must be prepared not to be virtuous." A good leader must "know how to do evil."

WONDER WHY?

Do you agree that it is safer for a leader to be feared than loved? Can you think of leaders who are effective without being feared?

Some of the other principles Machiavelli spelled out included the following.

+ People are "fickle, hypocritical, and greedy."

+ "Politics have no relation to morals."

+ "It is much safer to be feared than loved, if one of the two has to be wanting."

+ "(W)ar is not . . . to be avoided, but is only deferred to your disadvantage."

+ "Men should be either treated generously or destroyed, because they take revenge for slight injuries—for heavy ones they cannot."

+ "A prince never lacks legitimate reasons to break his promise."

PUBLICATION OF THE PRINCE

While Machiavelli lived, *The Prince* was an untitled manuscript that got passed around, copied, and read by a good number of people. But it was not called *The Prince* until it was published in 1532, five years after Machiavelli died.

Connections in Rome

When Machiavelli found himself out of work, he sought help from a friend in Rome named Francesco Vettori (1474–1539). Vettori was a fellow diplomat with close ties to the Medici family. The pope in 1513 was Pope Leo X (1475–1521), who was born Giovanni di Lorenzo de' Medici. Machiavelli hoped Vettori could put in a good word for him and find him a job at the Vatican.

When nothing panned out, Machiavelli sent a draft copy of *The Prince* to Vettori. He asked for his advice. Should he send it along to the Medici family? Vettori stalled for weeks before he finally gave Machiavelli an answer. He suggested Machiavelli keep the work to himself.

> "During the fifteen years that I have been studying the art of the state I have neither slept nor fooled around, and anybody ought to be happy to utilize someone who has so much experience."
>
> **MACHIAVELLI IN A LETTER TO VETTORI, DECEMBER 1513**

Lucrezia Borgia
By Bartolomeo Veneto (1470–1531), sixteenth century

LUCREZIA BORGIA (1480–1519)

Lucrezia Borgia was one of Pope Alexander VI's children. He used her, as he did her brother Cesare, to promote the family's rise to power. For Borgia, that meant enduring a series of three arranged marriages to powerful men. Her life was not easy. Borgia's first marriage ended when her father annulled it. Her second marriage ended when her husband was found strangled in his bed. Fortunately for Borgia, she thrived in her third marriage to Alfonso d'Este (1476–1534), the duke of Ferrara. A humanist scholar, Borgia spoke several languages, was a patron of the arts, and was a capable administrator who assisted in governing Ferrara. Borgia died at age 39, two days after giving birth to her 10th child.

Cover page of 1550 edition of Machiavelli's Il Principe *and* La Vita di Castruccio Castracani da Lucca

The Between Time

More than eight years passed between the time Machiavelli wrote *The Prince* and when he found regular work again with the Medici—but he still couldn't work for them in Florence. How did he spend all that time? He worked on the family's farm in Sant' Andrea. He played cards with the locals at a nearby inn. When he could, he joined fellow humanists for regular discussions of philosophy, literature, and history.

He also did a lot of writing. In addition to *The Prince*, Machiavelli wrote poetry, plays, and histories. One of his plays even made him a celebrity. *Clizia* was a comedy based on a play by the Roman playwright Plautus (died 185 BCE). When Machiavelli's *Clizia* was performed in 1525, it drew huge crowds. People talked about it for weeks.

Presenting *The Prince*

Machiavelli did eventually present a copy of *The Prince* to a member of the Medici family. In 1516, he dedicated a copy of the manuscript to Lorenzo di Piero de' Medici (1492–1519), then ruler of Florence and the duke of Urbino. He presented the book at court, but it made little impression upon Lorenzo.

Machiavelli gave *The Prince* to Lorenzo at the same time that another visitor gave the Florentine ruler two hound dogs. Of the two gifts, Lorenzo seemed much more enthusiastic about the dogs.

Working for the Medici

It was not until 1520 that the Medici family finally gave Machiavelli some work. Pope Leo X hired Machiavelli to write a history of Florence, even though Machiavelli still could not work in Florence. The Medici family extended its power to many parts of Europe, not just Florence!

Two people from the Medici family were popes during Machiavelli's lifetime: Pope Leo X and Pope Clement VII. Two more Medicis were even popes during the next century! Twenty years after Machiavelli died, Catherine de' Medici became queen of France, and later, Marie de' Medici was also queen of France!

"Everybody hated (Machiavelli) because of *The Prince*. The good thought him sinful, the wicked thought him more wicked . . . than themselves, so that all hated him."

GIOVAN BATTISTA BUSINI, QUOTED BY ROBERTO RIDOLFI (1531–1612), *THE LIFE OF NICCOLÒ MACHIAVELLI*

A portrait of Lorenzo di Piero de' Medici, circa 1450

By Raphael

Bad Prince vs. Good Prince

Many people who read *The Prince* agree with English historian Lord Macaulay (1800–1859). He described it as the work of a "fiend."

A sample of people known to have turned to *The Prince* for advice might seem to support that opinion. Two of history's most inhumane dictators, Adolf Hitler (1889–1945) and Joseph Stalin (1878–1953), kept *The Prince* on their nightstands.

But so have musicians, such as the rapper 50 Cent (1975–), and military leaders, such as former British Army officer Tim Collins (1960–). When Collins was at war in Iraq in 2003, he carried *The Prince* with him at all times.

WONDER WHY?

Would you like to read *The Prince*? Do you think you would find it useful? Why or why not?

Collins said it helped him come up with winning strategies for dealing with enemies and friends alike. "For good or for ill," Collins said, "this is what works."

Machiavelli's Legacy

What about Machiavelli himself?

He has been called a lot of bad things, including "devil" and "monster." Nothing indicates, however, that Machiavelli was ever terribly "Machiavellian." He was certainly an influential person for the 15 years that he served as second chancellor. But he never sought power for power's sake alone, and every devious strategy he described in *The Prince* was based on the actions of others.

WORDS OF WONDER

What vocabulary words did you discover? Can you figure out the meanings of these words by using the context and roots? Look in the glossary for help!

assassination · city-state · controversial
diplomat · Machiavellianism · moral

Machiavelli's tomb at
Santa Croce, Florence, Italy

"So great a name [has]
no adequate praise."

INSCRIPTION ON MACHIAVELLI'S TOMB

No matter how we feel about Machiavelli today, the originality of *The Prince* will remain his lasting legacy. *The Prince* truly was a new kind of mirror book, one that Machiavelli held up to the face of the Renaissance. His mirror showed what Renaissance politics really looked like, not what anyone wished it to be.

CONNECT

Watch this 60-minute documentary about Machiavelli.

🔍 BBC Imagine: Who's Afraid of Machiavelli?

Popularity for Princes

In *The Prince*, Machiavelli advised leaders that they need to be liked by the people they rule. He wrote, "[T]he best fortress you can have is in not being hated by your subjects." Do you think this is true? Let's do some research on what makes a good ruler.

> **What kinds of actions do leaders take to gain the support of their people?**

> **Conduct internet and library research on a historical leader who was known, at least at one point, to be liked by the people he ruled.** If you have trouble thinking of a figure to investigate, do an internet search for "great leaders in history" or brainstorm some ideas with classmates and friends.

> **Create a written or visual presentation that includes the following information:**

- A brief biography, including name, birth and death dates, where and how long the person ruled
- Some of the challenges the leader confronted

- Three to five things the leader did that gained them favor
- How long the leader lasted. Did the leader leave voluntarily or was the leader forced out? When and why did the leader lose support?

> **When you're done, compare your results among classmates and friends.** What similarities and differences do you see among various leaders? Do you detect any patterns of behavior? Do any economic or political conditions make it more likely that people will accept a leader's rule?

Can Bad Be Good?

Have you ever heard the saying that "The ends justify the means?" Machiavelli never used those exact words, but he did agree with their sentiment. He wrote time and again that it was okay for princes to do bad things if, in so doing, they accomplished something good.

Do you agree? Is it ever okay for leaders to do bad things if they end up doing something good?

> ➤ **Form two teams and prepare to debate the issue.** Both teams should provide examples from history to support their arguments.

> ➤ **Team A should prepare to offer three to five reasons why it is never okay for leaders to do bad things.**

> ➤ **Team B should prepare to offer three to five scenarios in which it is okay for leaders to do bad things if such actions result in a greater good.**

> ➤ **When your research is done, stage a friendly debate in front of classmates or friends.** When all the evidence has been heard, does a clear winner emerge? Which team presented the strongest arguments? Did you change your own mind based on what you learned? Why or why not?

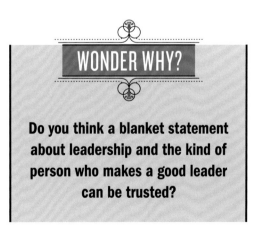

WONDER WHY?

Do you think a blanket statement about leadership and the kind of person who makes a good leader can be trusted?

CHAPTER 3

THOMAS
More

Thomas More was a Renaissance humanist who believed that education and rational thought could improve people's lives. He put his beliefs into practice, too. He educated his daughters and helped to found St. Paul's School in London, England. He even wrote a book, *Utopia*, which showed what a society ruled by rational thought might look like.

A medallion of Sir Thomas More

FAST FACTS

BIRTH DATE: 1478

PLACE OF BIRTH: LONDON, ENGLAND

AGE AT DEATH: 57

PLACE OF BURIAL: CHURCH OF ST. PETER, LONDON

FAMOUS ACCOMPLISHMENTS:
- LORD CHANCELLOR OF ENGLAND UNDER KING HENRY VIII
- COFOUNDER OF ST. PAUL'S SCHOOL IN LONDON
- *UTOPIA*

Thomas More was also deeply religious. Reading the non-Christian writings of ancient Greeks and Romans caused some Renaissance humanists to question the authority of the Catholic Church. But these writings never had that effect on Thomas More. In fact, he chose to die rather than renounce the Catholic Church.

Early Years

Thomas More grew up among the busy streets of London and amid the material comforts of a well-to-do family. His father, Sir John More (1451–1530), was an attorney who climbed to the highest levels of his profession. He provided his family with a large home in a section of the city that exposed More to the varied spectacles of Renaissance Europe. Royal processions passed near his home, while executions were carried out nearby as well.

Thomas More and extended family, circa 1593–94

By Rowland Lockey

Like many children of his time, More was familiar with death. He was the second of six children born to his mother, Agnes (dates unknown), but he was only one of three who survived beyond childhood. From 1479 to 1481, three of More's younger siblings died as a result of childhood illnesses. In 1499, he lost his mother as well.

A Saintly Namesake

More's parents named their first son after the English Catholic saint Thomas Becket (c. 1120–1170). As archbishop of Canterbury, Becket had taken religious actions that had gone against the will of the king of England, Henry II (1133–1189). Men loyal to Henry II assassinated Becket for defying the king.

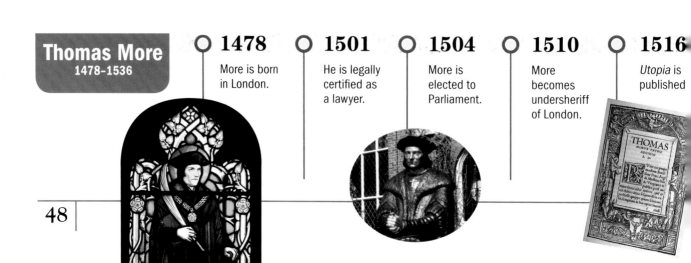

Thomas More
1478–1536

1478 More is born in London.

1501 He is legally certified as a lawyer.

1504 More is elected to Parliament.

1510 More becomes undersheriff of London.

1516 *Utopia* is published

On his way to school each morning, More walked by Thomas Becket's birthplace. Only it was no longer a house—it was the Saint Thomas of Acre Catholic Church.

> **"If honor were profitable, everybody would be honorable."**
>
> **THOMAS MORE**

1521
More becomes Henry VIII's secretary.

1529
He becomes lord chancellor of England.

1536
More dies by beheading in London for refusing to renounce his faith.

1886
In death, More is beatified by the Catholic Church.

1935
More is canonized by the Catholic Church.

A Renaissance Education

Thomas More followed in his father's footsteps and became a very successful lawyer. At the height of his career, he was lord chancellor of England, the highest civil post in the country. As lord chancellor, More served as a lawyer to King Henry VIII (1491–1547).

To arrive at that position required 16 years of education. More's schooling can be divided into four stages:

+ Five years of grammar school, from age 7 to 12

+ Two years as a page in the home of John Morton (1420–1500), one of the most powerful men in England. Morton was both the archbishop of Canterbury, the highest religious position in the country, and lord chancellor.

+ Two years at Oxford University, from age 14 to 16

+ Seven years of legal training

Lambeth Palace from the West, 1802. Thomas More served here as a page to John Morton for two years.

By Daniel Turner (1744-1844)

More started his schooling at a grammar school called Saint Anthony's. Here, he studied Latin. In fact, throughout More's 16 years of school, Latin was often the focus of his education. Why? Latin was the language of educated people throughout Europe. Books were written in Latin long before they were written in or translated into an author's native language, such as English or Italian. To know what was happening in science, mathematics, religion, or law, you had to read Latin.

Oxford University

credit: Tejvan Pettinger (CC BY 2.0)

CONNECT

Listen to this Harvard University commencement speech in Latin with English subtitles. Many of the English words we use today have Latin roots. Do any of the words in the speech sound familiar?

 **Harvard 2014 Latin**

At Saint Anthony's, boys participated in debates that were conducted in Latin. But the debates didn't take place at the school. They took place on raised platforms set up on the streets of London. In the neighborhood where More grew up, enough people knew Latin for these debates to be a popular form of entertainment.

After grammar school, as one of John Morton's pages, More continued his formal studies with a tutor. He also worked as a server at formal dinners. That's where he learned the courtly manners and refined forms of speech of the ruling classes of Europe. Those skills served him well as he progressed through his career.

At Oxford University, More followed a course of studies known as the "liberal arts." In 1490s Europe, that meant he studied the writings of ancient Greek and Roman philosophers.

You might imagine More doing a lot of reading. But that is not quite right. Books were still extremely rare in the Renaissance. Students could not own individual copies of all the books they were required to study. To learn, students had to listen.

WONDER WHY?

What difference would it make in your own education if you did not have easy access to books and material on the internet? How hard would it be for you to learn by having books read aloud to you in class? Do you think you could do it?

In class, professors recited from the works of scholars such as Aristotle and Cicero. After reading a passage aloud, the professor discussed it at length. After class, students discussed the passage among themselves, but without the book in hand as a reference.

Listening closely and remembering what he had heard were crucial elements of More's education.

The Dialectical Method

The goal of a liberal arts education was not to make students memorize a lot of facts and figures. The real objective was to train them in what was called the dialectical method. Students were constantly engaged in debates about what the ancient writers had said. The aim of their debates was to determine the truth.

For example, in *The Republic*, written in 381 BCE, Plato made the following statement: "The object of education is to teach us to love what is beautiful." The professor would discuss the topic. Students would later debate the issue among themselves. Was Plato's statement true or false? Speaking in Latin, students argued the case back and forth, testing the strengths and weaknesses of each other's reasoning. Do you ever do this in your classroom?

That is the dialectical method.

> **"An absolutely new idea is one of the rarest things known to man."**
>
> **THOMAS MORE**

More learned the law the same way that he learned the dialectical method. He listened to lectures, engaged in debates, and observed court proceedings. His success depended on two things. He had to recall English laws without referring to books and he had to present convincing oral arguments in public.

A statue of Thomas More in London

Making the World a Better Place

Renaissance humanists read ancient texts for guidance about how to live their own lives and how to improve their own societies. They turned to the past partly because they wanted to make things better in the present.

People in the Middle Ages and the Renaissance cared very much about what would happen to their souls after they died. They also cared about what happened in the world around them. Many people believed that their actions in the world would affect them in the afterlife, so they tried to give to charity and be good people.

As a humanist Christian, Thomas More believed people could—and should—try to make the world a better place. In his book, *Utopia*, he showed them how.

Writing *Utopia*

More began writing *Utopia* in 1515, when he was on a diplomatic trade mission in Flanders, in what is today known as Belgium. Talks among the ambassadors had stalled. With time to kill, More occupied himself by writing.

What he produced was a work of satirical fiction that people still read today.

You will be disappointed, however, if you expect *Utopia* to read like a modern-day novel. It does not. *Utopia* has just three characters and features almost no action, no plot, and no character development.

Why? Because More wrote *Utopia* as if he were transcribing a debate! He had been brought up on the dialectical method, and that was the model he turned to when he sat down to write a work of fiction.

Like most of More's writing, *Utopia* was composed in Latin and intended for an educated audience. The book was not translated into English, and so was not available to a larger audience until 1551.

The Utopian Lifestyle

Life in Utopia is described by a character named Raphael Hythlodaeus. A seaman who traveled the world, Hythlodaeus spent five years living among the Utopians. Of all the countries he had visited, he considered Utopia the best.

MARGARET MORE ROPER (1505–1544)

Thomas More believed in educating girls. In his home, he supervised the education of his own three daughters, plus two adopted daughters. More's eldest child, Margaret, took full advantage of that rare educational opportunity. A dedicated student, Margaret became what many people called the most educated woman in England. Margaret read and translated Greek and Roman texts, and once even participated in a philosophical debate as entertainment for Henry VIII. She was the first non-royal woman in England to publish an English translation of a Latin work—*A Devout Treatise upon the Paternoster.* The book was written by her father's friend, the humanist philosopher Desiderius Erasmus (1466–1536).

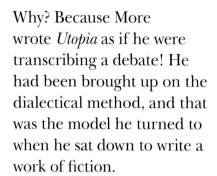

Portrait of Margaret More Roper, circa 1536

By Hans Holbein the Younger

> ## "What you cannot turn to good, you must at least make as little bad as you can."
>
> **FROM *UTOPIA*, BOOK 1**

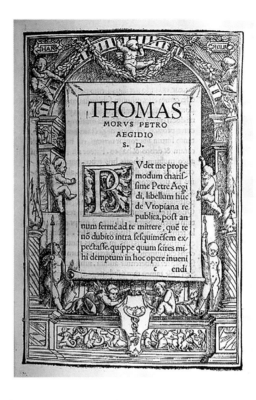

A 1518 edition of *Utopia*

What was Utopia like?

+ Anything you needed was given to you free of charge.

+ No one owned their houses. In fact, every 10 years, Utopians moved into a different house.

+ Everyone dressed the same.

+ Meals were eaten in large dining halls.

+ Everyone was trained to do a job and worked six hours a day.

+ Jobs people didn't like were rotated— everyone took a turn for a few months.

+ People received free medical care.

+ Criminals were punished by being forced into slavery.

+ Men stayed in the same neighborhood throughout their lives. Women had to move when they married.

+ Overpopulation was solved by colonizing other countries. If a country tried to force the Utopians out, the Utopians considered that cause for war.

+ Reading was the main recreational activity.

+ People were free to worship as they pleased.

+ Lawyers were not allowed on the island.

+ Gold and silver were nearly worthless. The Utopians used the metals to make chamber pots and chains for their slaves.

WONDER WHY?

Would you want to live in More's Utopia? Why or why not? In what ways does it seem like a good place? In what ways does it not?

Legacy of *Utopia*

Since its first printing in 1516, *Utopia* has been widely read and debated. The most perplexing question has always been: Did More really believe that *Utopia* represented an ideal society? Or did he mean it as a joke, as a form of satire?

> "Every utopia . . . faces the same problem: What do you do with the people who don't fit in?"
>
> **MARGARET ATWOOD (1939–), CANADIAN WRITER**

More left few clues about his true intentions, and scholars continue to debate *Utopia* to this day.

What's clear, however, is that *Utopia* had a lasting effect on literature. Before More, the word "utopia" was not even part of the English language. More's original definition of the word was "nowhere." During the last 500 years, however, utopia has come to signify any type of ideal society. Since the 1600s, many writers have used fiction to put forth their visions of a perfect world.

More's Legal Career

More wrote a great deal in his spare time, but he earned his living as an attorney. At the height of his career, from 1529 to 1532, More served as lord chancellor for King Henry VIII. In essence, More was the lawyer who oversaw all of the king's legal affairs.

WONDER WHY?

Today, authors more commonly write books about dystopian societies. These are worlds that are not perfect. Why do you think that is? Have you read any dystopian works of science fiction?

Later, he was one of several lawyers who worked for the king as members of his privy council, along with a number of very important noble men. That was where More won the trust of the king. Even before More was officially made lord chancellor, Henry VIII considered More the wisest of all his legal advisors.

Humanist Circles

Throughout his adult life, More was at the center of a network of people who believed in and explored the ideas of humanism. These were people such as the Englishman John Colet (1467–1519). Colet was the dean of St. Paul's Cathedral and the man with whom More helped found St. Paul's School. Their shared goal was to provide an education that combined the wisdom of the Christian faith with the wisdom of the ancient philosophers.

***Portrait of Erasmus*, 1523**

By Hans Holbein

***Sketch of John Colet*, circa 1535**

By Hans Holbein

More was also a close friend of Desiderius Erasmus, known as the "prince of the humanists." Born in Rotterdam in the Netherlands, Erasmus devoted his life to studying and writing.

He was staying at More's home when he composed what is considered one of the most important works of the Renaissance era—*In Praise of Folly*. In this work, Erasmus took a humorous approach to old superstitions and corruption in the Catholic Church. He dedicated this essay to More.

Thomas More and Henry VIII

To serve his king as lord chancellor was an honor, and More began his work with Henry VIII with high hopes.

More had known Henry VIII when he was a child, and he admired the young king for his physical strength, intelligence, and spirituality. Like More, Henry VIII was a devout Catholic. Pope Leo X himself referred to him as "Defender of the Faith." Henry VIII was also something of a humanist scholar.

> **"I do not care very much what men say of me, provided that God approves of me."**
>
> **THOMAS MORE, LETTER TO ERASMUS, 1532**

So More had many reasons to believe that his work with Henry VIII would go well. But he was tragically mistaken. His three years as lord chancellor, from 1529 to 1532, were filled with legal and religious struggles. They would eventually send More to an early grave.

WHO MAKES THE RULES?

Thomas More lived in a patriarchal society where men were in charge of almost everything. A big part of why Henry VIII wanted a son was that women were less valued than men, and people didn't want to have a queen ruling the kingdom. But it wasn't like that everywhere. Had More been born into the Mosuo tribe along the border of China and Tibet, the tables would have been turned. He would have found himself in a matriarchal society where the women were very much in charge.

Mosuo women ruled supreme in their homes and families. They restricted men to taking care of livestock and fishing, while they took care of everything else. They made up the rules about marriage, which included not having to live with their husbands. They also maintained exclusive control over their children. The Mosuo still survive today. They are considered the last true matriarchy in the world.

The King's Divorce

The problem was that the king wanted a divorce. His first wife had not provided him with a male heir, and he wanted to marry someone else, someone who could give him a son. To do that, he needed a divorce. The only person who could give Henry VIII a divorce was the pope, Clement VII (1478–1534), and there wasn't much chance that the pope would do it.

The situation was a terrible dilemma for More. As a Catholic, he sided with Clement VII and objected to the divorce. But as the king's attorney, he was expected to present the king's case to the pope.

More did what his job required, but it wasn't enough. Clement VII refused to grant Henry VIII a divorce.

The King's New Religion

Henry VIII was not a man to accept defeat. If the pope would not grant him a divorce, he would find another way to get it. His solution was to break with the Catholic Church altogether. If Henry VIII stopped being a Catholic, the pope would have no authority to tell him what to do.

Henry VIII formed a new church, which he called the Church of England. He made himself the head of the church, granted himself a divorce, and married Anne Boleyn (1501–1536).

By 1534, Henry VIII was not only king of England. He was also the spiritual leader of his people. Almost overnight, the Catholic Church no longer officially existed in England.

A portrait of Henry VIII, circa 1497
By Hans Holbein the Younger

CONNECT

What kind of person develops a new religion simply so he can get a divorce? Find out in this video.

🔍 mini biography Henry VIII

> "I die the king's faithful servant, but God's first."

MORE'S LAST WORDS BEFORE HE DIED, ACCORDING TO PARIS NEWSLETTER, AUGUST 4, 1535

The King's Loyalty Pledge

It wasn't that simple, of course. The Catholic Church was interwoven into people's lives. Even people who were loyal to Henry VIII were not likely to stop following in their faith just because the king told them to. To bend people to his will, Henry VIII would eventually order the destruction of England's Catholic churches and monasteries and make it a crime to follow the Catholic faith.

But in 1534, Henry VIII's first concern was to bring the people closest to him in line with the new order. He demanded that high-ranking English Catholics sign an oath affirming him not only as their king but as their spiritual leader. Anyone who refused to sign could be accused of treason.

Death and Sainthood

A steadfast Catholic, More refused to sign the king's oath. He would pledge spiritual loyalty to no one but the pope.

More resigned his job as lord chancellor. He retreated to his country estate, hoping that would be the end of his troubles. But Henry VIII would not let the matter rest. He accused More of treason. More was tried, convicted, and sentenced to death. On July 6, 1535, he was beheaded in a public execution.

For their loyalty to the pope, More and 52 other English Catholics were later made saints of the Catholic Church.

Tower of London, where More was imprisoned for several months before his execution

credit: Peter Pikous (CC BY 2.0)

More's Legacy

Thomas More lived by his convictions. He believed that girls deserved a solid education, so he educated his daughters. He believed Christians had much to learn from the ancient Greeks and Romans, so he helped found a school that educated children in both disciplines. He believed nothing was more important than his loyalty to the Catholic Church, so he chose death over disloyalty.

Today, More is admired by Catholics who revere him as a saint. He is also admired by non-Catholics for the intelligence, creativity, and dignity with which he lived his life.

Scholars may never decide if More truly believed that *Utopia* represented a better world than the one in which he actually lived. One thing is certain, however: More believed in trying to make his world a better place.

A painting of Thomas More saying goodbye to his daughter after his sentencing

By William Frederick Yeames (1835–1918)

WORDS OF WONDER

What vocabulary words did you discover? Can you figure out the meanings of these words by using the context and roots? Look in the glossary for help!

debate · dialectical method · rational
renounce · satire · treason

Utopia in Real Life

Thomas More wrote about a perfect place, but he never set out to create a real-life utopia. However, others have. Have you ever wanted to create the perfect society?

➤ **With an adult's permission, conduct internet and library research on a utopian community from the past or the present.** Consider the following.

· When and where was the community started?

· Who started it and why? What did they hope to accomplish?

· Is the community still in existence? If not, how long did it last?

· What challenges did the community face?

· Was it a successful community? Why or why not?

➤ **Now try to create plans for your own utopian community.** What will your community be based on? Will you have rules? What rules will you have? Who is allowed to join? How will you handle conflict?

➤ **Present your plans to a friend or classmate.** Try to sell them on the idea of joining your utopia. Does it work? Do you think utopian communities are worth striving for? Why or why not?

The museum at Fruitlands, a utopian society founded by Charles Lane and Amos Bronson Alcott (father of writer Louisa May Alcott) in the 1840s. This utopian society only lasted seven months.

What Does that Mean?

In 1515, Thomas More came up with a new word—*utopia*. In 2017, Merriam-Webster added more than 1,000 new words to its English language dictionary. Ten of those new dictionary entries are listed below.

> ➤ **Write down what you think each word means.** Then, with an adult's permission, check the actual definitions online.

Verbs	Nouns	Adjectives
· Face-palm	· Listicle	· Woo-woo
· Ghost	· Ping	· Seussian
· Photobomb	· Train wreck	
	· Side-eye	
	· Snollygoster	

> ➤ **Were your definitions close to the real thing?** Did you already know what some of the words meant? If you did, where had you encountered them or what clues made it possible for you to figure out what they mean?

> ➤ **Young people often come up with slang terms.** Do you use any slang words among your friends that your parents don't use? What communication need do they fill? Do you think the new words will last? Will people still be using them, like *utopia*, hundreds of years from now? Why or why not?

CONNECT

How does a word get into the dictionary? Who decides which new words are worthy of the dictionary? Learn all about the process from an editor at Merriam-Webster!

🔍 **Merriam-Webster new words**

NICOLAVS COPERNICVS.

Line engraving of Nicolaus Copernicus
credit: Wellcome Collection gallery (CC BY 4.0)

CHAPTER 4

NICOLAUS
Copernicus

Statue of Copernicus in Warsaw, Poland

By Bertel Thorvaldsen

Being a scientist during the Renaissance could be a lonely business. There were no graduate students to hang out with, no research institutes to work at, and no conferences to attend. It must have been especially lonely for the astronomer Nicolaus Copernicus.

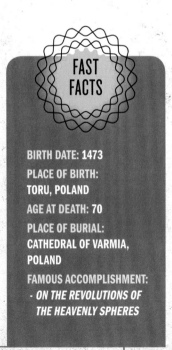

FAST FACTS

BIRTH DATE: 1473

PLACE OF BIRTH: TORU, POLAND

AGE AT DEATH: 70

PLACE OF BURIAL: CATHEDRAL OF VARMIA, POLAND

FAMOUS ACCOMPLISHMENT:
- *ON THE REVOLUTIONS OF THE HEAVENLY SPHERES*

Early in his career, he figured out a way to prove that the earth rotates around the sun. This was a huge accomplishment. For centuries, people had considered it a fact that the sun rotated around the earth. Through his observations and mathematical calculations, Copernicus cast a whole new light on the workings of the universe.

Did Copernicus spread the news? Did he share his findings with as many people as possible? He did not. In fact, he kept them a secret almost until the day he died.

Why? Because he didn't want to be laughed at and he didn't want to be accused of a crime.

> **"What could be more beautiful than the heavens, which contain all beautiful things?"**
>
> **COPERNICUS**

Early Years

The first 10 years of Copernicus's life are something of a mystery.

He was the youngest of four children born to Mikolaj Kopernik (dates uncertain) and Barbara Watzenrode (dates uncertain). The family lived on Saint Anne's Lane in Torun, Poland. But it's not until Copernicus turned 10 that his life came into focus. In 1483, Copernicus's father died, and he and his three siblings went to live with their maternal uncle, Lukasz Watzenrode (1447–1512).

What became of the children's mother? We can't say. Her date of death is uncertain. She may have died either before or after their father. Either way, Copernicus was adopted by his mother's brother. Watzenrode had a comfortable career in the Catholic Church, and he provided for all four of the Kopernik children.

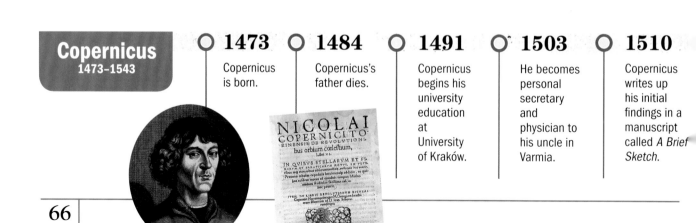

Copernicus
1473–1543

1473
Copernicus is born.

1484
Copernicus's father dies.

1491
Copernicus begins his university education at University of Kraków.

1503
He becomes personal secretary and physician to his uncle in Varmia.

1510
Copernicus writes up his initial findings in a manuscript called *A Brief Sketch*.

Becoming an Astronomer

Copernicus attended three different universities, was a student for more than 10 years, but never got a degree in astronomy—because astronomy degrees didn't really exist!

When he was 18, he studied at his uncle's old school, the University of Kraków in Poland. From there he went to Italy. First, he studied Church law at the University of Bologna, and then he studied medicine at the University of Padua.

A statue of Copernicus in Poland

NAME CHANGES

Throughout his lifetime, the scientist we call Copernicus was known by several names. He was christened with the Polish name of his father—Mikolaj Kopernik. But when he was a child, he went by the German version of his name—Niklas Kopernik. When he became a scholar writing in Latin, Mikolaj/Niklas Latinized his last name to Copernicus.

1539
Georg Joachim Rheticus begins to work with Copernicus in Varmia.

1540
Rheticus publishes *A First Account*, outlining Copernicus's work.

1543
On the Revolutions of the Heavenly Spheres is published in April.

1543
Copernicus dies of a stroke on May 24.

1822
The Catholic Church formally accepts a heliocentric model of the cosmos.

2010
The Polish people honor Copernicus with a second funeral.

Where and when did astronomy figure into his education? That was in Bologna, where he took astronomy classes from Professor Domenico Maria Novara (1454–1504) and also became his assistant. Copernicus was so hooked on astronomy that he rented rooms in Novara's house so they could study the night sky together.

From then on, watching the heavens became Copernicus's lifelong obsession.

> **"It is the duty of the astronomer to compose the history of the celestial motions through careful and expert study."**
>
> **COPERNICUS**

FAMILY AFFAIRS

Copernicus never married and never had any children, but he was still part of a family. He had three older siblings—a brother Andreas, and sisters Barbara and Katharina. Two of his siblings settled into careers with the Catholic Church. Andreas became a canon, just like Copernicus. Barbara became a nun. Only Katharina married. She gave birth to five children. After she died at a young age, Copernicus financially supported his orphaned nephews and nieces for the rest of his life.

Jagiellonian University, formerly the University of Kraków

credit: Jennifer Boyer (CC BY 2.0)

Earning a Living

Copernicus paid for his school by becoming a low-level official with the Catholic Church, and he even earned a degree in Church law by passing an exam when he was 30 years old. He returned to Poland and went to work as the personal physician and secretary to his uncle, Lukasz Watzenrode.

Frombork Cathedral, where Copernicus served as canon and where he is buried

credit: Mathiasrex (CC BY 2.5)

Watzenrode had risen steadily within the Catholic Church, becoming the bishop of Varmia in Poland in 1489. Watzenrode helped his nephew find success in the Church as well. He paved the way for Copernicus to become the canon of Varmia in 1510.

As canon, Copernicus was an administrator who oversaw thousands of acres of land owned by the Church. Peasants lived and worked on the land, and they paid rent, plus a portion of everything they made, to the Church. For his work, Copernicus was provided with an income, servants, and a place to live.

WONDER WHY?

What financial and educational advantages made it possible for Copernicus to pursue his interest in astronomy? What circumstances would have made it more difficult for him to succeed?

Our Place in the Universe

For thousands of years, humans assumed the earth was a stationary object that sat at the center of the cosmos. The earth stood still while the heavens rotated around it. The logic was straightforward. People saw the sun rise in the east and set in the west every day.

But there was a hitch. Anyone who watched the sky closely knew that not all astronomical bodies circled the earth once a day. Some planets inched across the sky in one direction for weeks, only to switch course and go back to where they had started.

An explanation for those wandering planets eluded astronomers for centuries.

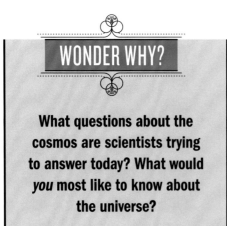

WONDER WHY?

What questions about the cosmos are scientists trying to answer today? What would *you* most like to know about the universe?

The Geocentric Universe

Claudius Ptolemy (circa 100–170 CE) thought he had figured out the cosmos. A Greek astronomer who lived in Alexandria, Egypt, Ptolemy imagined the cosmos as a series of nested spheres. The earth sat still at the center, while everything else orbited the earth in spheres that had depth, width, and height. He speculated that as planets moved in a circle around the earth, they also moved within the space of their individual spheres.

Most astronomers doubted that heavenly bodies wandered around inside those Ptolemaic spheres. But since no one could come up with a better model, they stuck with it

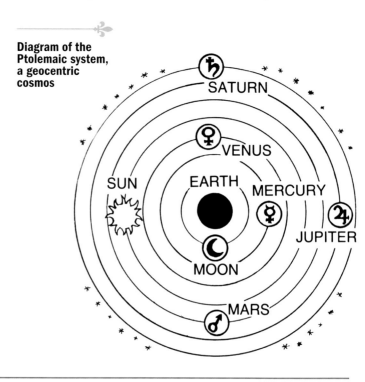

Diagram of the Ptolemaic system, a geocentric cosmos

SATURN
VENUS
SUN
EARTH
MERCURY
MOON
JUPITER
MARS

The Heliocentric Universe

The unsolved problems with Ptolemy's theory troubled Copernicus. He and many other astronomers believed that heavenly bodies moved in uniform ways. He rejected the notion that they wandered off course within a defined sphere.

It's not clear when exactly Copernicus reimagined the Ptolemaic cosmos, but he began to share writings about it with friends by 1514. Going on little more than an educated guess, he imagined a cosmos where the sun was the center of the universe.

Copernicus still suspected the universe was made up of a series of spheres. But he proposed that the six known planets circled the sun in a predictable manner based on the speed of their revolutions. The fastest-revolving planet was closest to the sun and the slowest-revolving planet was farthest from the sun. They lined up in this order: Mercury, Venus, Earth, Mars, Jupiter, and Saturn.

"[A]s soon as . . . people realize . . . I attribute certain (heavenly) motions to the globe of the Earth, they will at once clamor for me to be hooted off the stage . . . ."

COPERNICUS, *ON THE REVOLUTIONS*

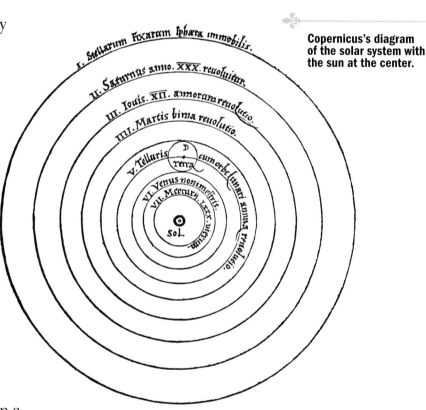

Copernicus's diagram of the solar system with the sun at the center.

CONNECT

Watch this video to learn more about Copernicus and his diagram of the universe.

🔍 **Copernicus beauty of diagrams**

Copernicus's Joke

Copernicus came up with one of the greatest scientific discoveries in human history. Even to educated people, the idea that the earth was moving seemed ridiculous. Copernicus did not want to be made fun of, so he shared his ideas with only a few friends.

But people laughed at him just the same. When Copernicus wrote up his ideas in a booklet that he gave to a friend, the manuscript was copied and passed around. Soon, people joked that Copernicus had mistaken the earth for a side of beef and set it roasting on a spit beneath the sun.

OTHER PLACES, OTHER PEOPLE

Throughout history, people from around the world have studied the night skies. The ancient Polynesian peoples, for example, were intimately familiar with the stars. They were a seafaring people and great explorers who used the stars to guide them thousands of miles across the Pacific Ocean. The basic principle behind celestial navigation lies in understanding where a star sets in relation to where it rises in the sky. Like the sun (which is also a star), stars rise in the east and set in the west, 180 degrees opposite from where they rose. As Polynesian navigators came to recognize stars, they were able to figure out both where they were and which direction they were headed.

Learn more about how Polynesians navigated by the stars.

🔍 KHON2 News Hokulea

> **"I have kept (my findings) suppressed and hidden . . . for almost four times nine years already."**
>
> **COPERNICUS, *ON THE REVOLUTIONS***

Science and Religion

Of greater concern to Copernicus, however, was the Catholic Church. The Church very much cared about correctly understanding astronomy, but religious leaders also needed to make sure that whatever theories people came up with fit with the Bible and the writings of the Church fathers. These were people such as Augustine, Ambrose, and Jerome who wrote after the Bible was finished and helped people interpret it.

One of the reasons that the Church cared about astronomy was that it had to create a calendar so that holidays happened at the right time. By 1513, people at an important council in the Church noticed that the shortest day of the year wasn't actually the shortest day of the year! They had been using a calendar that was just a tiny bit incorrect. It said that the year was 365.25 days, when we now know it is 365.2422 days!

Anonymous painting of Savonarola's execution, 1650

"You expect . . . to hear from me how it entered my mind to dare . . . to imagine some motion of the Earth."

COPERNICUS, *ON THE REVOLUTIONS*

Why would such a small difference matter? Well, after 1,500 years, the calendar was wrong by almost 12 days, and that's a big difference!

In 1513, the Church didn't know the correct length of the year, but they knew that the calendar was wrong. They asked astronomers to find the right length, and in the process accidentally encouraged people to study and make observations that led to proof that the earth revolves around the sun. These observations led to arguments between the Church and scientists, and these arguments continued for centuries. It can be very difficult to convince someone that the world doesn't work the way they think it works!

Copernicus continued his work in secret.

BEFORE COPERNICUS

Copernicus was not the first person to suggest that the earth orbited the sun. That distinction goes to a Greek known as Aristarchus of Samos (c. 310–230 BCE). Aristarchus's original texts have never been found, but both the man and his idea of a heliocentric universe are mentioned in the works of other ancient writers. Copernicus certainly knew about Aristarchus. He even mentioned him in a first draft of *On the Revolutions*, but the reference was removed in the final edition of the book.

❈❈❈❈❈❈❈❈❈❈❈❈❈❈❈❈❈❈❈❈❈❈❈❈❈❈❈❈❈❈❈❈❈❈

Mathematics and Astronomy

Proposing that the earth orbits the sun was a radical notion. But as we have seen, Copernicus was not the first person to come up with that idea. Actually, quite a few Renaissance scholars had similar thoughts as well. They just didn't want to talk about it, partly because they didn't know how to prove that what they suspected was true.

That's where Copernicus was different. He proved that the heliocentric model was correct. He backed up the theory with mathematical equations. In fact, much of *On the Revolutions* is composed of page after page of equations.

To most people, those equations were bewildering. That's why Copernicus's book included a warning: "Let no one untrained in geometry enter here." But for people trained to read the universal language of higher mathematics, *On the Revolutions* was perfectly clear. Copernicus had proved that the sun was the center of the universe.

Tools of the Trade

Copernicus made his discoveries with just his eyes and three mechanical instruments.

✦ Triquetrum. Used since ancient times, a triquetrum allows astronomers to determine the altitude of heavenly bodies.

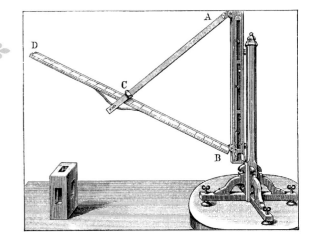

Triquetrum

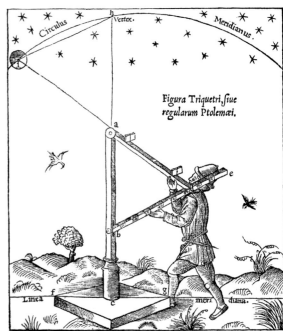

Triquetrum being used by an astronomer, 1544

By Orontii Finaei

Ptolemy using a quadrant

Artist unknown, 1564

✦ Quadrant. An ancient instrument used to measure angles of up to 90 degrees.

✦ Armillary sphere. A model of objects in the sky, an armillary sphere is a framework of rings that represent the lines of celestial longitude and latitude.

Armillary Sphere

CONNECT

Watch an explanation of how the planets really move!

🔍 **SciShow Copernicus**

FEMALE COMPANIONS

Copernicus was never known for having affairs or fathering any children, but he did get into trouble for hiring female housekeepers. He was suspected of having a long-term relationship with one servant in particular, Anna Schilling (dates unknown). Her presence in the Copernicus household was deemed scandalous enough for a bishop to have her legally banned from Varmia.

Publishing Copernicus's Theory

When Copernicus was 66 years old, a young mathematician and astronomer from Wittenberg, Germany, entered Copernicus's life. His name was Georg Joachim Rheticus (1514-1574). He arrived, unannounced, at Copernicus's house, determined to meet the man who had developed a heliocentric model of the universe. Rheticus urged Copernicus to publish his findings.

Title page from the second edition of *De Revolutionibus Orbium Coelestium*, 1566

CONNECT

Want to learn more about the solar system? Try this video from National Geographic!

🔍 **Solar System 101 Nat Geo**

Then, he stayed with Copernicus for two years to help the older man compile his theories, observations, and mathematical tables into a book called *On the Revolutions of the Heavenly Spheres*. During those two years, Rheticus also wrote a small book of his own.

In *A First Account*, published in 1540, Rheticus outlined the basics of Copernicus's revolutionary model of the cosmos. Rheticus's book was widely read. It paved the way for the publication of Copernicus's own work in 1543.

> **"If what I am now saying is obscure, it will nevertheless become clearer in its proper place."**
>
> **COPERNICUS, *ON THE REVOLUTIONS***

Changing Minds

Copernicus died of a stroke before *On the Revolutions of the Heavenly Spheres* was published, so he never faced the ridicule of other scientists or condemnation by the Catholic Church. Both things happened once his ideas became known.

As time passed, however, Copernicus was proven right. In the seventeenth century, the German astronomer Johannes Kepler (1571–1630) proved mathematically that planets travel in elliptical orbits.

Also in the seventeenth century, the Italian astronomer Galileo Galilei (1564–1642) developed telescopes powerful enough for astronomers to see for themselves that Copernicus's heliocentric model was accurate.

Sadly, the religious debate lasted longer, and it was Galileo who suffered from the Church's disapproval. In 1633, the Catholic Church convicted Galileo of heresy for promoting a heliocentric model of the universe. His punishment was to live under house arrest until the day he died.

Portrait of Johannes Kepler by an unknown artist, 1610 (left)
Portrait of Galileo Galilei by Justus Sustermans, 1636 (right)

Astronomer Copernicus, or
Conversations with God

By Jan Matejko, 1873

WONDER WHY?

Why do you think it took people
so long to accept Copernicus'
heliocentric model of the universe?
Are there any scientific discoveries
that people find hard to accept today?

"[W]hatever appears as a motion
of the sun is really due rather
to the motion of the Earth."

COPERNICUS, *ON THE REVOLUTIONS*

Statue of Maria Cunitz in Swidnica, Poland

credit: Sueroski (CC BY 3.0)

MARIA CUNITZ (1610-1664)

Maria Cunitz was one of the few women of the Renaissance to earn a reputation as a scientist. Like Copernicus, Cunitz was born in Poland. Unlike Copernicus, she never attended university—because women were not allowed to attend universities! She was educated at home, presumably by her father, who was a doctor. No matter how she came by her knowledge, Cunitz added to our understanding of the solar system. In 1650, she published *Urania Propitia*, a book that simplified mathematical calculations known as the Rudolphine Tables. These were complex algorithms written by the astronomer Johannes Kepler in 1627 that dealt with the motions of the planets. Cunitz's simplifications made Kepler's algorithms more accessible to a wider audience. In honor of her work, a crater on Venus and a minor planet are named after Cunitz.

> "I think the first necessity is for us to examine carefully what is the relationship of the Earth to the heavens."
>
> **COPERNICUS, *ON THE REVOLUTIONS***

Copernicus's Legacy

Today, Copernicus takes his place as one of the most influential scientists in human history. He is also a cultural hero to the Polish people. When he died in 1543, Copernicus was buried in an unmarked grave under the floor of the cathedral where he served as canon.

On May 22, 2010, however, the Polish people gave Copernicus a second funeral. They dug up his remains and laid them to rest in a memorial tomb that the public can visit.

WORDS OF WONDER

What vocabulary words did you discover? Can you figure out the meanings of these words by using the context and roots? Look in the glossary for help!

celestial · geocentric · heliocentric heresy · sphere · universe

Project

Observe the Night Sky

An introduction to astronomy is as easy as opening your eyes. Astronomers actually encourage new stargazers to familiarize themselves with the night sky with their own eyes before they use a telescope. Try it and see what you spot!

> **Schedule three to five nights in a row when you can observe the night sky.** Follow the tips below. Regardless of where you live, you can study certain features in the sky.

- Get up high. Look for a spot that provides an unobstructed view.

- Avoid lighted areas. Avoid streetlights, illuminated buildings, and vehicle headlights. Hint: If there is too much light for you to see the stars, study the moon instead.

- Use a red flashlight. A red light is best for finding your way without adding too much light. Hint: Wrap a flashlight or your cell phone in red tissue paper.

- Let your eyes adjust. It may take a few minutes for your eyes to adjust to the dark.

- Brave the cold. Clear, crisp, winter nights are best.

- Avoid full moons. The light of a full moon makes it harder to see the stars.

- Use an app. Free star charts and other apps show in real time what you should see according to where you are.

> **Write down a detailed observation of what you see in the sky each night.** What changes do you notice over the course of a few nights? Does the night sky start to seem more familiar to you? Why or why not? What challenges did you encounter in your observations? Did this activity increase your curiosity about celestial bodies? Can you imagine becoming as familiar with the stars as the ancient Polynesian navigators or Copernicus?

CONNECT

Want a closer look? Learn how to build a simple telescope.

🔎 **YouTube build a telescope**

What Good Is Math?

Mathematics was a crucial part of Copernicus's scientific research. Without the ability to prove the heliocentric theory mathematically, his work would not have progressed beyond an educated guess. Mathematics remains a cornerstone of scientific research today. But the study of advanced mathematics also has many applications outside the laboratory.

➤ **With an adult's permission, conduct internet and library research on careers in mathematics.** Create a written or visual presentation about what you discover. Your presentation should answer the following questions.

· How many careers in mathematics did you find?

· Did you understand what all the jobs would involve? Were there some that you had to investigate further to understand what they were?

· Can you calculate the average annual salary, across multiple jobs, for a career mathematician?

· What did you discover that surprised you?

· Did you find a job as a mathematician that interests you? Why or why not?

Try This!

➤ **Conduct an interview with a professional mathematician.** You might find one at a local university or engineering company. What kind of math does their job require? Do they use math every day? What would they like young people to know about the role of math in our lives?

CONNECT

Learn more about how mathematics is the language of the universe.

 BBC maths language universe

Portrait of Sir Francis Bacon
By an unknown artist,
circa 1731

CHAPTER 5

FRANCIS
Bacon

Francis Bacon's contribution to the Renaissance is often underappreciated. His most important ideas were ignored during his own lifetime. And even now that they have been accepted, it's easy to forget that he thought them up in the first place. So what did Francis Bacon do?

Francis Bacon at 18 years old
By Nicholas Hilliard

FAST FACTS

BIRTH DATE: 1561

PLACE OF BIRTH:
LONDON, ENGLAND

AGE AT DEATH: 65

PLACE OF BURIAL:
ST. MICHAELS CHURCH, SAINT ALBANS, IN HERTFORDSHIRE, ENGLAND

FAMOUS ACCOMPLISHMENTS:
 - **DEVELOPED THE ENGLISH ESSAY**

 - **FATHER OF THE SCIENTIFIC METHOD**

 - **AUTHOR OF *ATLANTIS***

Bacon outlined an approach to scientific inquiry that changed more than just one branch of science—his ideas changed science itself. Francis Bacon laid the groundwork for the scientific advancements that define our modern age.

Early Years

Francis Bacon grew up in a family steeped in power and intellectual prominence. His father, Nicholas Bacon (1510–1579), was an attorney who rose to the highest civil position in the country. He was lord keeper of the Great Seal (similar to lord chancellor) to Queen Elizabeth I (1533–1603).

As a child, Francis Bacon met Queen Elizabeth I enough times for her to give him a nickname. Impressed with the boy's intelligence, she referred to him as her "Little Lord Keeper."

His uncle, William Cecil (1520–1598), was even closer to the queen. He served as her chief advisor for 40 years. He had more input into Elizabeth's decision-making than nearly anyone else.

The young Bacon lived around a kind of intellectual royalty as well. His mother was Anne Cooke (1528–1610), the daughter of a humanist scholar who had once been a tutor to a future king. She spoke Greek, Latin, and Italian, and helped to educate Bacon at home for the first 12 years of his life.

Bacon
1561–1626

1561
Bacon is born at York House in London.

1605
He publishes *On the Advancement of Learning.*

1606
Bacon marries Alice Farnham and later is appointed solicitor general.

1607
Bacon writes *Thoughts and Conclusions on the Interpretation of Nature.*

1613
He is appointed attorney general.

Portrait of Sir Nicholas Bacon

Artist Unknown

Studies Abroad

Poor health kept Francis largely at home for more than a decade. But homeschooling didn't hinder his academic progress. At age 12, along with his older brother Anthony Bacon (1558–1601), Francis enrolled as a student at Cambridge University. At age 14, he tagged along with Anthony to study law.

1617
Bacon is appointed lord chancellor.

1620
Bacon publishes *New Method*.

1621
Fortunes come crashing down when he is convicted of bribery.

1622
Bacon publishes *History of Henry VII*.

1626
Bacon dies of pneumonia.

1627
New Atlantis is published.

Portrait of Sir Amias Paulet, English ambassador to France between 1576 and 1578

By Nicholas Hilliard

Within just a few months, however, the two brothers parted ways. Anthony continued his law studies in London. Francis, then 15, set off for an extended visit abroad. He left with Amias Paulet (1532–1588), the English ambassador to Paris. Bacon's formal studies continued with tutors, but for the next three years, he also worked as Paulet's assistant.

Bacon traveled with Paulet not only to France, but also to Spain and Italy. This was a rare opportunity. It gave Bacon a front row seat inside the royal courts of Europe.

WONDER WHY?

Many American college students spend a semester studying in a foreign country. How does that enhance their education? Is it something you would like to do? Even if you don't attend college, would you like to travel abroad? Why or why not?

Reversal of Fortune

Given the many advantages he grew up with, Bacon must have looked forward to a promising future. But in 1579, he was dealt a setback that would affect him for the rest of his life.

That year, his father died unexpectedly, cutting short Bacon's travels with Paulet. When Bacon returned to London, he received more bad news. His father had died without having created a will that provided for the financial security of his youngest son.

Gray's Inn, where Bacon studied law

That meant the bulk of the family fortune was inherited by Bacon's older brother, Anthony.

At age 18, Bacon still had a lot going for him. He was smart and he knew people in high places. But without the safety net of his family's money, Bacon realized that he would have to survive on his wits.

"Believing I was born for the service of mankind . . . I set myself to consider in what way mankind might be best served, and what service I was myself best fitted by nature to perform."

BACON, PRIVATE DOCUMENT DISCOVERED AFTER HE DIED

Moving Forward

After the death of his father and the loss of his financial support, Bacon settled down to finishing his education. Just like his father, he became an attorney. He also hoped to find work in the court of Elizabeth I—just like his father,

Given his intelligence and his family connections, it seemed a reasonable expectation that the queen would offer a job to her former "Little Lord Keeper." But try as he might, Bacon repeatedly failed to secure an important position in the queen's government.

> "[B]y far the greatest obstacle to the progress of science . . . is found in this—that men despair and think things impossible."
>
> **BACON,** *NEW METHOD*

He advanced nicely in his law career and also served as a member of Parliament. But it took two decades, and the death of Elizabeth I, before Bacon received his first significant court appointment. When Bacon was 45 years old, King James I (1566–1625) tapped him to be his solicitor general.

WONDER WHY?

What is revealed about Bacon's character because he never gave up on finding work in the English royal court? Do you think he was proud, stubborn, persistent, or something else?

Family Affairs

Bacon had about as much bad luck in his romantic relations as he had in his career. When he was 36 years old, he had his heart set on marrying Elizabeth Hatton (1578–1646). A young widow, Elizabeth had all but promised to marry Bacon when she suddenly dropped him for someone else.

Another nine years passed before Bacon found someone else. And when he did marry, his bride, Alice Barnham (1592–1650), was a 14-year-old girl. That seems shocking today—a 45-year-old man marrying a teenager! But at the time, such age differences were not unusual.

> "The human mind and its management is ours to improve.
> There are no insuperable objects in the way; simply it
> lies in a direction untrodden by the feet of men."

BACON, *THOUGHTS AND CONCLUSIONS*

Letters from that time period reveal that Bacon was often the subject of cruel gossip, but no evidence suggests that anyone criticized his marriage to Alice.

Bacon and his wife had no children.

BACON AND SHAKESPEARE

Francis Bacon was one of the most prolific and gifted writers of his time. Indeed, Bacon was such a talented writer, a theory developed in the nineteenth century that he was the real author behind the plays of William Shakespeare (1564–1616). Why would anyone think that? First, people speculated that Shakespeare could not possibly have written everything for which he was given credit. They wondered if he had some help. Second, a close analysis of Bacon's and Shakespeare's writing reveals some striking similarities. If Shakespeare did have some help, Bacon seemed a likely candidate. Today, most scholars conclude that Shakespeare did, in fact, write all the works that bear his name. But the conspiracy theory lives on. Only Bacon has been replaced by another candidate—Edward de Vere, Earl of Oxford (1550–1604).

Creating the Essay

When you have to write an essay, you can thank—or blame—Francis Bacon. He was the first English writer to explore a broad range of subjects in the short format that became the essay.

Bacon also wrote with a less ornamental style of writing than was common. His prose was elegant and precise—exactly the qualities your English teacher is looking for in the papers you write!

Portrait of William Shakespeare, 1610

By John Taylor

Portrait of Edward de Vere

Artist Unknown

Philosopher of Science

It took Bacon 20 years to obtain the kind of position he thought he deserved. But he was never an idle man. He progressed in his career as a lawyer. He served as a member of the House of Commons—one of the houses of Parliament (the English version of U.S. Congress). And he wrote constantly—books, poetry, essays, histories, letters, fiction, and more.

WONDER WHY?

What kind of science have you studied in school? Why is it important for even young children to learn about biology, chemistry, and more?

"Now the true and lawful goal of the sciences is none other than this: that human life be endowed with new discoverie and powers . . . ."

BACON, *NEW METHOD*

Science was one of Bacon's favorite topics. He was passionate about how the untapped potential of the human mind and the natural world could improve people's lives. In several books, he outlined a comprehensive new approach to scientific inquiry.

The Scientific Method

How can we know when we have gotten to the truth of something? That was the question Francis Bacon explored in his book *Novum Organum* (*New Method*, in English). Published in 1620, *Novum Organum* laid out an approach to discovering the truth about the world we live in.

The Baconian method, as it was called, can be summed up in five steps.

+ Make an observation.

+ Ask a question.

+ Form a hypothesis, or an educated guess.

+ Conduct an experiment.

+ Analyze the results.

If you have participated in a school science fair, you may ask yourself: so what? These days, what Bacon proposed can seem pretty obvious.

Frontispiece of
New Method

> "A new world beckons. The trial should be made. Not to try is a greater hazard than to fail."
>
> **BACON, *THOUGHTS AND CONCLUSIONS***

But in 1620, scientific experiments were usually validated by being observed by gentlemen and other people of high status. Bacon's push for a rigorous approach to scientific discovery was new. Today, we conduct experiments like Bacon proposed, and then we confirm that the experiments were done correctly with peer review— when other experts look at the experiment and agree that it was done correctly.

> "[Bacon] was a creature of incomparable abilities of mind, of a sharp and catching apprehension, large and faithful memory, plentiful and sprouting inventions, deep and solid judgment . . ."

TOBIE MATTHEW (1577–1655), PREFACE TO HIS PUBLISHED LETTERS

Bacon was the first person to map out a system of experimentation that would lead to reliable results.

In Support of Science

In another book, *On the Advancement of Learning,* Bacon explored numerous ways to support scientific efforts and to pass knowledge on to future generations. His suggestions included these ideas.

✦ Universities should conduct scientific research.

✦ College professors should be paid more.

✦ Researchers should form professional associations, share their ideas, and help one another to determine the validity of their results.

CONNECT

Learn more about Francis Bacon in this mini-biography!

🔍 **Cloud Bio Francis Bacon**

OTHER PLACES, OTHER PEOPLE

Francis Bacon was the first Westerner to really encourage a systematic approach to scientific research. But throughout history, Europeans were not always at the forefront of scientific and technological advances. Indeed, compared to the achievements among ancient Chinese cultures, Europeans were frequently far behind. For example, included among China's many scientific achievements are what historians sometimes refer to as the "four great inventions." These are paper making, printing, the compass, and gunpowder. Innovations in these areas led to dramatic social change in Europe. Hundreds of years passed, however, between the time the Chinese first developed them and when they found their way out of Asia.

✦ The results of scientific research should be published and made available to the public.

✦ Government should support scientific research.

As with Bacon's description of the scientific method, these ideas may not seem new today. But in 1604, they were revolutionary.

Portrait of Maria Sibylla Merian, circa 1700

By Jacobus Houbraken

Bacon in Disgrace

By the time Francis Bacon turned 60, he had achieved a great deal. He had been knighted and made a lord and a viscount. He even followed in his father's footsteps to become lord chancellor. But his time at the top was short-lived. Soon after he was appointed lord chancellor, Bacon was accused of bribery.

Rather than fight the charges, Bacon admitted guilt to more than 20 counts of bribery. As punishment, he was briefly imprisoned in the Tower of London. Upon his release, he was barred for life from ever working for the English government.

> "It is this glory of discovery that is the true ornament of mankind."

BACON, *THOUGHTS AND CONCLUSIONS*

He lived for five years after his release from the tower, struggling to support himself by his writing. He died of pneumonia in 1626, greatly in debt.

MARIA SIBYLLA MERIAN (1647–1717)

In *New Method*, Francis Bacon stressed that the first job of scientists was to make precise observations. No scientist lived up to that standard better than Maria Sibylla Merian. A Dutch citizen trained as an artist by her father, Merian forged a career as a world-class natural illustrator. She traveled on expeditions to places as far away as Suriname and published engravings of plants, animals, insects, and more. As a scientist-illustrator, Merian performed groundbreaking work with insects. Before Merian, few people gave insects much thought. Now, it's a whole branch of science known as entomology. Merian studied insects in detail, becoming one of the first naturalists to observe them directly. She eventually described the life cycles of 186 insect species.

GIFTS VS. BRIBES

As lord chancellor, Bacon undoubtedly accepted gifts from the people he did business with. But, as with his marriage to a much younger woman, the practice was not unusual for a man in his position. Bacon swore many times that the gifts he accepted did not influence the legal decisions he issued as lord chancellor. Historians have mostly agreed that Bacon was not a corrupt lord chancellor. Most likely, the bribery charges were brought against him by political rivals wanting to get him out of office.

Bacon's Legacy

Francis Bacon died before any of his ideas about scientific research were given serious consideration. But since his death, nearly all of Bacon's ideas have been adopted.

WONDER WHY?

Are you interested in scientific research? What discoveries would you like to make? What advances do you hope others are working on?

The Baconian method evolved into the scientific method. It is the foundation of modern scientific research.

Every branch of science has peer-reviewed journals where new findings are published and debated. Major universities support important scientific research. Governments routinely fund research that benefits the common good.

"I consider (Bacon one of) the three greatest men that have ever lived, without any exception, and as having laid the foundation of those superstructures which have been raised in the Physical and Moral sciences."

THOMAS JEFFERSON (1743-1826), LETTERS

NEW ATLANTIS

Like Thomas More, Bacon wrote a fictional story about a perfect world. In *New Atlantis*, Bacon created the utopian island of Bensalem. The country was populated with pious Christians who had received their Christian texts directly from God, but in Bacon's ideal world, science held a place that was just as important. The heart of Bensalem society was a place called Solomon's House. It was Bacon's vision of a modern research institute. Experiments were conducted according to the Baconian method, and all research was geared toward improving peoples' lives. Unfinished at the time of his death, *New Atlantis* was published in 1627, a year after Bacon died.

Memorials to Francis Bacon have been erected all over the world. But the greatest tribute of all may be that we practically take his great ideas for granted. They have become a permanent part of the way we think and order our lives.

WORDS OF WONDER

What vocabulary words did you discover? Can you figure out the meanings of these words by using the context and roots? Look in the glossary for help!

bribery · hypothesis · intellectual
prolific · scientific method

Science Gone Wrong

When scientific research is conducted properly, we can trust that the results are valid. But what happens when scientific research is *not* undertaken in a rigorous and reliable manner?

➤ **With an adult's permission, conduct internet and library research to learn about a scientific endeavor that was conducted in a way that led to invalid results.** Create a written or visual presentation of your research. Your presentation should answer the following questions.

- What were the researchers trying to discover? What problem were they trying to solve?
- When and where did the research take place?
- In what way were their methods not aligned with acceptable scientific standards?

- Were the researchers deliberately ignoring acceptable scientific standards? Were they just not good at what they were doing?
- Did their faulty methods have an impact on the general public? If so, how were people affected?
- After the botched research became public knowledge, were any new laws or rules enacted to prevent similar things from happening again?

➤ **Share and discuss your presentations among classmates or friends.** What similarities and differences do you see among several examples of scientific research gone wrong?

Scientific Advances: Blessing or Curse?

Francis Bacon believed that scientific research, when properly conducted, would benefit the human race. Almost 400 years after his death, do you think he was correct? On the whole, have scientific advances been good or bad for humankind?

> **Set up a debate among your friends or classmates to discuss that question.** One group will do research to argue that scientific advances have benefited humans. The other group will conduct research to support the opposite stance—that scientific advances are harming humans.

> **Each side should come up with three to five historically factual examples to support their opinion.**

> **Stage your debate among classmates or friends.** Then discuss the final outcome. Can one side be declared a winner? Why or why not? Did you learn anything that influenced the way you think about scientific advances in the modern age?

Try This!

> **What happens when people are suspicious of the scientific process and its results?** For example, there are families who choose not to vaccinate children, even though many rigorous scientific studies have been done that show the benefits of vaccination on both individuals and the general population. Why do you think people remain unconvinced about the usefulness of vaccinations? Can you think of other examples like this? Try to find a common cause behind this phenomenon.

administrator: a person responsible for running a business or organization.

adorn: to decorate something.

algorithm: a step-by-step procedure for solving a complex problem.

altitude: the height of an object above sea level.

ambassador: someone who represents his or her country.

annul: to declare that a marriage is no longer legal.

antiquity: something from ancient times.

apprentice: a person who learns a job or skill by working for someone who is good at it.

architect: a person who designs buildings.

architecture: the style or look of a building.

arranged marriage: a marriage where parents decide who their children will marry for political or economic reasons.

assassination: murder committed for political rather than personal reasons.

astronomer: a person who studies the stars, planets, and other objects in space.

astronomical: having to do with astronomy or the study of space.

astronomy: the study of the sun, moon, stars, planets, and space.

baptize: to make a person an official member of a specific church or religion.

beatify: to declare something to be holy.

BCE: put after a date, BCE stands for Before Common Era and counts years down to zero. CE stands for Common Era and counts years up from zero. This book was published in 2018 CE.

biology: the science of life and living things.

blockade: a way to prevent people or things from entering or leaving a specific place.

bribery: to give money or favors to someone in power so they will grant special treatment.

brothel: a house where men pay money to have sex with women.

bubonic plague: a deadly infectious disease carried by rats and mice that can spread to humans. Also called the Black Death.

buttress: a support in a building that projects out from a wall.

canon: an administrator for the Catholic Church.

canonize: to declare a person a saint.

celestial: positioned in the sky or outer space.

chamber pot: a large, bowl-shaped pot used as an indoor toilet.

chemistry: the science of how substances interact, combine, and change.

Christian: a person who follows the religion of Christianity. Its central belief is that Jesus Christ is the son of God.

circumference: the distance around the edge of a circle.

circumnavigation: traveling completely around something, such as the earth.

city-state: a city and its surrounding area, which rules itself like a country.

civil: non-military and/or non-religious.

collage: a work of art made up of different pieces of material.

colony: a group of people who form a settlement in a distant land, but remain under the control of the government of their native country.

condemnation: strong disapproval.

condottiere: a leader or a member of a troop of mercenaries.

continent: one of the earth's large landmasses, including Africa, Antarctica, Asia, Australia, Europe, North America, and South America.

controversial: likely to cause the public to disagree and argue over something.

corrupt: behaving dishonestly for money or personal gain.

cosmos: the universe.

crops: plants grown for food and other uses.

culture: the beliefs and way of life of a group of people, which can include religion, language, art, clothing, food, holidays, and more.

debate: a discussion between people with differing viewpoints.

debt: a service or money owed.

defer: put off until later.

devious: underhanded, sly, treacherous.

devout: deeply religious.

dialectical: the logical discussion of opinions and ideas.

diameter: the distance across a circle through the middle.

dilemma: a situation in which a difficult choice has to be made.

diplomat: an official who represents a country in foreign political affairs.

duchy: the territory ruled by a duke or duchess.

dystopia: an imaginary place where things have gone terribly wrong.

elliptical: oval or egg shaped.

elude: to fail to be understood.

endeavor: an attempt to achieve a goal.

engineer: a person who uses science, math, and creativity to design and build things.

enhance: to make greater.

epitaph: an inscription on a grave that describes or is in memory of the person buried there.

era: a period of history marked by distinctive people or events.

eternal: lasting forever.

execution: carrying out the death sentence of a person found guilty of a crime.

exclusive: restricted or limited to a certain person, group, or area.

expedition: a difficult or long trip taken by a group of people for exploration, scientific research, or war.

fiction: stories that describe imaginary events and people.

GLOSSARY

Flanders: a region that is now part of the Netherlands, France, and Belgium.

flange: a projecting rim or rib on an object.

geocentric: a model of the universe, now disproved, with the earth at the center of the solar system.

geometry: the branch of math that looks at the relationship of points, lines, surfaces, shapes.

gilded: covered in gold.

heliocentric: a model of the solar system having the sun at the center.

heresy: having a belief that is not approved of by the Church.

horizon: the point in the distance where the sky and the earth (or the sea) seem to meet.

horizontal: straight across from side to side.

humanity: all people and the quality of being human.

humanism: a belief that human beings can improve themselves and their world through a rational approach to problem-solving.

humanist: a person who studies or supports humanism.

idle: not working.

illusion: a trick of the eyes that makes people see something differently than it really is.

influential: having a strong effect on another person.

inhumane: without compassion for misery or suffering.

innovation: a new invention or way of doing something.

insuperable: impossible to overcome.

intellectual: a person who is engaged in learning and thinking.

justice: fair action or treatment based on the law.

laborer: a person who does physical work.

legitimate: in agreement with rules or laws.

linear perspective: a technique used to portray three-dimensional objects on a two-dimensional surface.

livestock: animals raised for food and other products.

Latin: the language of ancient Rome and its empire.

latitude: imaginary lines around the earth that measure a position on the earth north or south of the equator.

literature: written work such as poems, plays, and novels.

longitude: imaginary lines running through the North and South Poles that indicate where you are on the globe.

Machiavellianism: a type of personality that includes deceit, cynicism, and manipulation, especially in politics.

manufacture: to make something by machine, in a large factory.

manuscript: a book written by hand.

mass produce: to manufacture large amounts of a product.

mathematician: an expert in math.

matriarchal: related to a society controlled by women.

GLOSSARY

medieval: from the Middle Ages.

mercenary: a hired soldier.

Mesopotamia: an area of ancient civilization between the Tigris and Euphrates Rivers in what is now called Iraq, Kuwait, and Syria.

Middle Ages: the period of time between the end of the Roman Empire and the beginning of the Renaissance, from about 350 to 1450 CE. It is also called the Medieval Era.

molten: metal, stone, or glass that has been liquefied by heat.

monastery: a community of monks bound by religious vows.

moral: related to what is wrong or right behavior.

mosque: a Muslim place of worship.

oath: a solemn promise.

obscure: not clearly understood.

oral: spoken.

orbit: the path of an object circling another in space.

Pantheon: an ancient Roman temple famous for its dome.

Papal States: territories in Italy under the direct rule of the pope between the eighth and nineteenth centuries.

Parliament: the law-making body of the British government.

patent: having the exclusive right to make, use, or sell something.

patriarchal: related to a society controlled by men.

patron: a person who gives financial support to a person or organization.

peasant: a farmer during the Middle Ages who lived on and farmed land owned by his lord.

peer review: the process by which scientific findings are judged by professionals in the same field.

philosopher: a person who studies knowledge, truth, and the nature of reality.

planet: one of the large celestial bodies that orbit around the sun.

Polynesian: relating to the people who inhabit the many islands of the South Pacific Ocean.

pope: the head of the Catholic Church.

population: the people of an area or country.

potential: something that is possible, or that can develop into something real.

precarious: dangerous or uncertain.

prestigious: something inspiring respect and admiration.

prolific: producing many works.

prose: written language in its ordinary form, writing that is not poetry.

pulley: a wheel with a groove for a rope used to lift a load.

quadrant: an instrument used to measure the height of the planets, moon, or stars.

radical: extreme, or a person with extreme political or social views.

101

rational: logical, not based on religion or superstition.

reasoning: the process of thinking about something in an intelligent way in order to make a decision or form an opinion.

Reformation: a religious movement beginning in 1500 that rejected the Catholic pope and established the Protestant churches.

Renaissance: the period of European history from the 1300s to the 1600s, which is marked by a flourishing of literature, art, exploration, and invention.

renounce: to formally reject a religion, idea, or position.

reputation: the beliefs or opinions that are generally held about someone or something.

revere: to honor and show respect.

revolution: one complete turn made by something moving in a circle around a fixed point.

rigorous: extremely thorough and disciplined.

ruse: a trick played on another person.

satire: humor used to exaggerate and reveal people's stupidity or political foolishness.

scientific method: a method to test a theory that involves observing, measuring, and testing data.

secular: not religious.

solar system: a family of eight planets and their moons that orbit the sun.

sphere: a round shape that looks like a ball.

spiritual: religious, relating to the soul or spirit.

stationary: not moving.

steadfast: firm and unwavering.

superstition: beliefs that deal with non-scientific things, such as good and bad luck.

systematic: done according to a plan.

technology: the tools, methods, and systems used to solve a problem or do work.

telescope: an instrument used to observe distant objects.

theorem: a logical rule in math.

transcribe: to write down.

treason: the crime of betraying one's country.

treatise: a philosophical or scientific exploration in writing of a particular subject.

uniform: always the same in character or degree.

universe: everything that exists, everywhere.

utopia: an imaginary place where things are ideal.

Vatican: the government offices of the pope in Rome.

values: strongly held beliefs about what is valuable, important, or acceptable.

vaulted: a building or room with an arched roof or roofs.

villa: a large and luxurious country home.

wits: smarts and brainpower.

RESOURCES

BOOKS

The Beginning of the Renaissance: History Books for Kids 9–12. Baby Professor, May 2017.

Ince, Elizabeth. *St. Thomas More of London.* Ignatius Press, February 2003.

Rockwell, Anne F. *Filippo's Dome.* Atheneum, 1967.

Sponsel, Heinz, and Gold, Monica (tr.). *Copernicus: Struggle and Victory.* AWSNA, August 2007.

Wagner, Heather Lehr. *Machiavelli: Renaissance Political Analyst and Author.* Chelsea House Publications, September 2005.

VIDEO

PBS: *Medici: Godfathers of the Renaissance* (DVD release date 2005)
Also available via Amazon Prime video streaming service

NOVA: *Great Cathedral Mystery* (DVD release date 2014)

A Man for All Seasons (DVD release date 2011)

MUSEUMS AND HISTORIC SITES

The Museums of Florence
www.museumsinflorence.com/musei/cathedral_of_florence.html

The Center for Thomas More Studies, University of Dallas, Dallas, Texas
www.thomasmorestudies.org

The Jagiellonian University Museum, Krakow, Poland
www.museums.krakow.travel/en/muzea/id,74,trail,16,t,the-jagiellonian-university-museum.html

The Copernicus House Museum, Torun, Poland
www.torun.pl/en/turystyka/zabytki/copernicus-house

RESOURCES

QR CODE GLOSSARY

PAGE 6: hrc.utexas.edu/exhibitions/permanent/gutenbergbible

PAGE 9: classics.mit.edu/Plato/republic.2.i.html

PAGE 13: youtube.com/watch?v=I1CaeatMdmU

PAGE 16: khanacademy.org/humanities/renaissance-reformation/early-renaissance1/beginners-renaissance-florence/v/linear-perspective-brunelleschi-s-experiement

PAGE 17: vimeo.com/195934650

PAGE 22: khanacademy.org/humanities/renaissance-reformation/early-renaissance1/sculpture-architecture-florence/v/brunelleschi-dome-of-the-cathedral-of-florence-1420-36

PAGE 26: youtube.com/watch?v=Pltw8GMNAqo

PAGE 27: thekidshouldseethis.com/post/step-into-a-summer-igloo-in-360-as-its-being-built

PAGE 32: youtube.com/watch?v=xuqPhR8QTZQ

PAGE 35: youtube.com/watch?v=Vufba_ZcoR0

PAGE 37: machiavellivilla.com/gallery.php

PAGE 43: youtube.com/watch?v=a0lfo_cWxQc

PAGE 51: youtube.com/watch?v=G5ARhxgODI4

PAGE 59: biography.com/video/henry-viii-mini-biography-126127683527

PAGE 63: youtube.com/watch?v=5EeQEqqj-dI

PAGE 71: youtube.com/watch?v=E6_j8Xv2ae0

PAGE 72: youtube.com/watch?v=dla3RoQo37M

PAGE 75: youtube.com/watch?v=khlzr6610cQ

PAGE 76: youtube.com/watch?v=libKVRa01L8

PAGE 80: youtube.com/watch?v=uZeF1KETaU4

PAGE 81: youtube.com/watch?v=hbDkSaSnbVM

PAGE 92: youtube.com/watch?v=PTpoGDnjXuk

INDEX